W9-BIX-306

The Collected Poems
of Lucille Clifton
1965–2010

The Collected Poems

of LUCILLE CLIFTON
1965–2010

■

Edited by Kevin Young and Michael S. Glaser
Foreword by Toni Morrison
Afterword by Kevin Young

american poets continuum series, no. 134

BOA Editions, Ltd. ■ Rochester, NY ■ 2012

First Edition
12 13 14 15   7 6 5 4 3 2 1

For information about permission to reuse any material from this book, please contact The Permissions Company at www.permissionscompany.com or e-mail permdude@eclipse.net.

The publication of this book was made possible in large part by the Lannan Foundation.

Publications by BOA Editions, Ltd.—a not-for-profit corporation under section 501 (c) (3) of the United States Internal Revenue Code—are made possible with funds from a variety of sources, including public funds from the New York State Council on the Arts, a state agency; the Literature Program of the National Endowment for the Arts; the County of Monroe, NY; the Lannan Foundation for support of the Lannan Translations Selection Series; the Mary S. Mulligan Charitable Trust; the Rochester Area Community Foundation; the Arts & Cultural Council for Greater Rochester; the Steeple-Jack Fund; the Ames-Amzalak Memorial Trust in memory of Henry Ames, Semon Amzalak and Dan Amzalak; and contributions from many individuals nationwide.

Cover Design: Daphne Morrissey
Cover Photo: AP Photo/Mark Linnihan
Interior Design and Composition: Richard Foerster
Manufacturing: Thomson-Shore
BOA Logo: Mirko

Library of Congress Cataloging-in-Publication Data

Clifton, Lucille, 1936–2010.
 The collected poems of Lucille Clifton 1965–2010 / edited by Kevin Young and Michael S. Glaser ; foreword by Toni Morrison ; afterword by Kevin Young. — 1st ed.
  p. cm. — (American poets continuum series ; 134)
 ISBN 978-1-934414-90-3 (hardcover : alk. paper)
 I. Young, Kevin. II. Glaser, Michael S., 1943– III. Title.
 PS3553.L45 2012
 811'.54—dc23
                                    2012014244

Lannan
BOA Editions, Ltd.
250 North Goodman Street, Suite 306
Rochester, NY 14607
www.boaeditions.org
A. Poulin, Jr., Founder (1938–1996)

State of the Arts

NYSCA

ART WORKS.
arts.gov

Contents

■ good news about the earth (1972)

about the earth

heroes

some jesus

■ Uncollected Poems (1973–1974)

■ an ordinary woman (1974)
sisters

■ two-headed woman (1980)

homage to mine

two-headed woman

the light that came to lucille clifton

■ **Next (1987)**

we are all next

or next

■ **The Book of Light (1992)**

■ Uncollected Poems (1993)

■ The Terrible Stories (1996)

1. A Dream of Foxes

2. From the Cadaver

3. A Term in Memphis

4. In the Meantime

5. From the Book of David

■ Blessing the Boats (2000)

new poems

■ Mercy (2004)

last words

stories

■ Voices (2008)

hearing

being heard

■ **Uncollected Poems (2006–2010)**
Book of Days (2006)

Last Poems & Drafts (2006–2010)

ma
mommy
grandma
lue

always light

Editors' Note

This volume represents all the poems Lucille Clifton published in book form during her lifetime. It also includes groupings of previously un-collected poems placed in the book roughly when they were written: first, a selection of "Early Uncollected Poems" from the many Clifton wrote and kept but did not gather in her first full-length book, *Good Times* (1969); second, we have included a recently discovered typescript, "Book of Days," that Clifton seems to have completed during 2006; and, finally, a grouping of "Last Poems & Drafts" that include late work and fragments, in various states of completion, found among her papers housed at Emory University. In all cases we have maintained the unique typography (and handwriting) found in her uncollected work.

We have not gathered here Clifton's few occasional poems—with rare exceptions, sprinkled as "Uncollected Poems" throughout—nor any poems she published in magazines but left uncollected in book form during her lifetime. This volume also does not include her powerful memoir, *Generations*, which may still be found in *Good Woman*, the first of her selected poems. We also do not include her many works written for children. A bibliography at the back of the book reveals the breadth of her literary production.

In all, the *Collected Poems* offers readers a sense of Clifton's poetic development from her earliest work to her last.

—Kevin Young & Michael S. Glaser

Foreword: Lucille Clifton

The love readers feel for Lucille Clifton—both the woman and her poetry—is constant and deeply felt. The lines that surface most frequently in praise of her work and her person are moving declarations of racial pride, courage, steadfastness or they are eloquent elegies for the vulnerable and the prematurely dead. She sifts the history of African Americans for honor:

> like my aunt timmie.
> it was her iron . . .
> that smoothed the sheets
> the master poet slept on . . .

She plumbs that history for justice:

> loaded like spoons
> into the belly of Jesus
> where we lay for weeks for months
> in the sweat and stink
> of our own breathing . . .
> can this tongue speak
> can these bones walk
> Grace Of God
> Can this sin live

From humor to love to rage, Clifton's poems elicit a visceral response. It would be difficult to forget the raucous delight of "wishes for sons":

> i wish them cramps.
> i wish them a strange town
> and the last tampon.
> i wish them no 7-11 . . .
>
> let them think they have accepted
> arrogance in the universe,
> then bring them to gynecologists
> not unlike themselves.

And the wide love on display in "libation" demands our own:

> i offer to this ground,
> this gin.
> i imagine an old man
> crying here
> out of the overseer's sight,
>
> pushing his tongue
> through where a tooth
> would be if he were whole.
> the space aches
> where his tooth would be,
>
> where his land would be, his
> house   his wife   his son
> his beautiful daughter . . .

Can any one of us not shiver with the tenderness in "miss rosie"?

> when I watch you
> wrapped up like garbage
> sitting, surrounded by the smell
> of too old potato peels

or
when I watch you
in your old man's shoes
with the little toe cut out
sitting, waiting for your mind
like next week's grocery
i say
when I watch you
you wet brown bag of a woman
who used to be the best looking gal in georgia
used to be called the Georgia Rose
i stand up
through your destruction
i stand up.

There is no mistaking the rage in "the photograph: a lynching":

is it the cut glass
of their eyes
looking up toward
the new gnarled branch
of the black man
hanging from a tree?

is it the white milk pleated
collar of the woman
smiling toward the camera,
her fingers loose around
a christian cross drooping
against her breast . . .

These are examples of the range and complexity of the emotions she forces us to confront. It is no wonder that her devoted fans speak often of how inspiring her poetry is—life-changing in some instances.

Accolades from fellow poets and critics refer to her universal human heart; they describe her as a fierce caring female. They compliment her courage, vision, joy—unadorned (meaning "simple"), mystical, poignant, humorous, intuitive, harsh and loving.

I do not disagree with these judgments. Yet I am startled by the silence in these interpretations of her work. There are no references to her intellect, imagination, scholarship or her risk-taking manipulation of language. To me she is not the big mama/big sister of racial reassurance and self-empowerment. I read her skill as that emanating from an astute, profound intellect—characteristics mostly absent from her reviews. The personal courage of the woman cannot be gainsaid, but it should not function as a substitute for piercing insight and bracing intelligence. My general impression of the best of her work: seductive with the simplicity of an atom, which is to say highly complex, explosive underneath an apparent quietude. The Lucifer poems alone belie this "down to earth" theme:

> come coil with me
> here in creation's bed
> among the twigs and ribbons
> of the past. i have grown old
> remembering this garden,
> the hum of the great cats
> moving into language, the sweet
> fume of man's rib
> as it rose up and began to walk.

That line, "come coil with me" says everything you need to know about Lucifer and his conversation with God.

> . . . let us rest here a time
> like two old brothers
> who watched it happen and wondered
> what it meant.

This is no good/evil cliché. This revelation embraces dichotomy and reaches for an expression of our own ambivalent entanglements. Similarly in "lucifer speaks in his own voice":

so am i certain of a
graceful bed
and a soft caress
along my long belly
at endtime . . .
i   the only lucifer
light-bringer
created out of fire
illuminate i could
and so
illuminate i did

The touch, the view, is outside Milton or Dante. Clifton's Lucifer is:

phallus and father
doing holy work . . .

if the angels
hear of this

there will be no peace
in heaven

Then there is the excellent "eve thinking." Not the mute, seductive
even corrupt Eve we are accustomed to. Clifton's Eve thinks!

it is wild country here
brothers and sisters coupling
claw and wing . . .

i wait
while the clay two-foot
rumbles in his chest
searching for language to

call me
but he is slow

tonight as he sleeps
i will whisper into his mouth
our names.

The last lines of "adam thinking" hit us with its sheer original-
ity:

this creation is so fierce
i would rather have been born

I crave a book of criticism on Lucille Clifton's work that scours it
for the meanings therein and the stone-eyed intellect on display.

I edited a book by Lucille. *Generations.* The only prose, I believe, she
ever wrote for publication. I was so pleased to be working with her
because, although we knew each other briefly at Howard University,
I had not seen her since then. The manuscript was impressive—hon-
est, clear-eyed with a shapeliness natural to poets. During one of our
conversations in my office she told me that she spoke fairly regularly
to her deceased mother. "Really? How?" I asked. "Prayer?" "No," she
said. "Ouija Board." I smiled, not with condescension, I hope, but
with fascination. "What does she say?" "Many things," she answered,
"though she has no sense of time. She speaks of things past as though
they were in the future. As in 'you are going to have two beautiful
daughters.' I tell her I already have beautiful daughters."
    Lucille continued, "But I get the impression she isn't very interested
in me. Once I asked her about something extremely important to me
and she said, 'Excuse me, I have to go. I have something to do.'"
    Something to do? I was mesmerized. The dead have active, curious,
busy existences? Lucille assured me it seemed to be so. I was happy
beyond belief to contemplate the afterlife that way. Not some static
hymnal-singing, self-aggrandizing chorus, nor blank preconscious-
ness—but life otherwise.
    Since that conversation it occurred to me what was so fetching
about *Generations*: in addition to possessing the ease and intimacy of
Clifton's poetry, it speaks to, for, and from fictional and posthumous

lives—Moses, Medgar Evers, Amazons, Bob Marley, Sleeping Beauty, etc. She is comfortable and knowing about the dead.

Perhaps I should dwell more on her famous, self-affirming

> won't you celebrate with me
> what I have shaped into
> a kind of life? . . .

Perhaps. But it is "in the evenings" that freezes my attention; it is "what did she know . . . ," "aunt jemima," "horse prayer," and others that tell us everything we need to know, streamlined and perfect.

> the air
> you have polluted
> you will breathe
>
> the waters
> you have poisoned
> you will drink
>
> when you come again
> and you will come again
>
> the air
> you have polluted
> you will breathe
>
> the waters
> you have poisoned
> you will drink

Lucille is another word for light, which is the soul of "enlightenment." And she knew it.

—Toni Morrison

Early Uncollected Poems

(1965–1969)

BLACK WOMEN

America made us heroines
not wives,
we learned the tricks
to keep the race together
but had to leave our men
to find themselves
and now they damn
what they cannot forgive.

Even ol massas son
lives in a dream
remembering the lie
we made him love.

America made us heroines
not wives.
We hid our ladyness
to save our lives

■

OLD HUNDRED

NOW LET US MAKE
    nobody knows
A JOYFUL NOISE
    under the cry
LET US SHOUT
    under the glistening
HALLELUJAH
    sleeps goodby
AND LET US MAKE
    God is a friend
A JOYFUL NOISE
    standing between
UNTO THE LORD
    what I've been told
AMEN   and the trouble I've seen.

■

THE OLD AVAILABLES HAVE

the old availables have locked the door.
goodby to friday open house
nobody enters friday anymore

the old availables have locked the door
goodby to chocolate open house
nobody enters friday anymore.

some of us are tired
and all of us a

all of us are tired
and some of us are mad

■

CHAN'S DREAM

When I was born
the red baby lions were asleep.
When I was born
they were dreaming in my body bed
and then the American Cowboy
saw where I was borning
and shot me
and the little red lions ran growling
kill the cowboy
kill the cowboy
kill the cowboy

■

from **Dark Nursery Rhymes for a Dark Daughter**

I

Flesh-colored bandage
and other schemes
will slippery into
all your dreams
and make you grumble
in the night,
wanting the world to be
pink and light.
Wherever you go,
whatever you do,
flesh-colored bandage
is after you.

III

Beware the terrible tricky three;
Blondy and Beauty and Fantasy.
Together they capture little girls
and push them into little worlds.
They might have had fun
if they had run
the first time that they heard them hiss
"Promises   promises   promissesss."

IV

Ten feet tall
or giant arm,
nobody has
your sunshine charm.

■

5/23/67
R.I.P.

The house that is on fire
pieces all across the sky
make the moon look like
a yellow man in a veil
watching the troubled people
running and crying
    Oh who gone remember now like it was,
    Langston gone.

■

ONLY TOO HIGH IS HIGH ENOUGH
for Charlie Parker

probably even Icarus, plummeting from
an impossible height
was proud
a man beset by feathers
wearing bird colors
hearing bird conversations plain
sharing bird ambitions
flying above the possibilities
pursuing with immortals
the pride of wings

■

THE COMING OF X

Disillusioned by bad dreams
and a country bent on evening
the dusky girls and brothers have
noticed the prevalence of black
bark   bird   berry   and
raised their feral shadows till
they walk like men to the slaughterhouse.

■

Conversation Overheard in a Graveyard

Harriet: This place has made us heroines
             not wives
             and kept us from its sparkles and
             its paints
             and made us dull in natural disguise.
Sojourner: We've lost our ladyhood
             but saved our lives.
Harriet: What mirror will remember you and me
             suckling strangers and sons?
Sojourner: History.

■

SUNDAY DINNER

One wants
in a fantastic time
the certainty of
chicken popping in grease
the truth of potatoes
steaming the panes and
butter
gold and predictable as
heroes in history
melting over all.

■

MY FRIEND MARY STONE FROM OXFORD MISSISSIPPI

We know we ought to be enemies,
her voice perhaps,
thirty three years off the Delta and
still caked in mud or
my hair perhaps,
bushed for the warrior women of Dahomey,
we know we ought to be enemies, only
Oh Mr. Faulkner
to prevail is such an awe full responsibility
to "have a spirit capable of compassion and sacrifice and
    endurance"
is an awe full responsibility but
we know we have to try it and
we are both trying to try it
we
red as the clay hills and blacker than loam
friends.

■

SPRING THOUGHT FOR THELMA

Someone who had her fingers
set for growing,
settles into garden.
If old desires linger
she will be going
flower soon. Pardon
her little blooms
whose blossoming was stunted
by rooms.

■

my mother teached me
and my father preached me
what is love.
there is no more to know.
except
as I lay quiet
cold as a rained on sidewalk
after my daughter's father
has teached me
and preached me
I can hear off in the nigger streets
laughing and cursing and
something like a cry

■

To Mama too late

The lady who is gone
had forgot all about
I love you.
If I had fastened it someplace
on to her midnight pillow
I might be able to say goodnight
and she might not be asleep.

■

Dear Mama,
    here are the poems
    you never wrote
    here are the plants
    you never grew,
    all that i am
    i am for him
    all that i do
    i do for you.

■

Dear
I have sent you your box
as promised
and hope you like it all
I put in tuna fish because
you like it   keep
your room clean (smile) and
we are all alright only
I misses you so much
my baby
don't fall in love with no
stranger
write when you have time and
be a good girl for your
                    Mama

■

Dear
it was a nice day today
Hills is pretty this time of year
though maybe not like D.C.
Everybody been so nice to me
since you been gone
Everybody say they will pray for you
to get good grades and
everything
I will close now as I am tired
write when you get time   we
buried your uncle this morning
and
be a good girl

Mama

∎

plain as a baby
my Mama would sit
in the chair by the window
(where she started dying)
and watch the weekends
awe full as China
and hum
            Take my hand
            Take my hand.
            Oh Precious Lord
my Mama sang

■

Everytime i talk about
the old folks
tomming and easying their way
happy with their nothing and
grateful for their sometime
i run up against my old black
Mama
and i shut up and stand there
shamed.

■

satchmo

he disremembers why he started grinning
this old great one
standing behind his cornet.
something to do with
new orleans as a girl
and the old men following death down rampart street.
he disremembers why, only now
always he comes with music
and with grinning
and we are glad
we swing with this old great one
who has something to do with life
grinning at love and death.

∎

FOR PRISSLY

girl
looking like a wild thing
if you keep on your loving way
if you don't stop caring and fearing
and noticing things
and understanding things
people gone call you crazy

■

the last Seminole is black

and rolls his own in a john
bargaining with his brain
for a reef of peace

smoking his way across the reservations
into a high and splendid
land of grass

nodding and smiling to hear the drums begin
and all the mighty nations celebrating
the endless littlebighorns
in his mind

■

a poem written for many moynihans

ignoring me
you turn into blind alleys
follow them around
to your boyhouse
meet your mother
green in her garden
kiss what she holds out to you
her widowed arm and
this is betterness

ignoring me
you make a brother for you
she drops him in the pattern
you made when you were sonning
you name her wife to keep her
and this is betterness

ignoring me
your days slide into seasons
you build a hole to fall in
and send your brother running
following blind alleys
turning white as winter
and this is
betterness

■

the poet is thirty two

she has such knowledges as
rats have,
the sound of cat
the smell of cheese
where the holes are,
she is comfortable
hugging the walls
she trembles over herself
in the light
and she will leave disaster
when she can.

■

QUOTATIONS FROM AUNT MARGARET BROWN

Abraham Lincoln
just like my Daddy;
dead.

White men
just walking all on the moon,
he go where he want to go.

Talk about Columbus,
I tell you who discovered
America;
Martin Luther King
that's who.

■

daddy
you whole old hoodoo man
you always knew everything
like when you said
them old white people
they don't mean you no good
and even
the time the light-skinned jimmy came by
and you looked at his three-button roll
and said
here's this nigger i don't like

■

take somebody like me
who Daddy took to sunday school
and who was a member of the choir
and helped with the little kids at
the church picnic,
deep into Love thy Neighbor   take
somebody like me
who cried at the March on Washington
and thought Pennsylvania was beautiful
let her read a lot
let her notice things
then
hit her with the Draft Riots and the
burning of the colored orphan asylum
and the children in the church and
the Lamar busses and
the assassinations and the
bombs and all the spittings on our
children and
these beasts were not niggers
these beasts were not niggers
she
will be too old to change and
she will not hate consistently   or long
and she will know herself a coward and
a fool.

■

let them say

that she had going for her
a good ass and six children.
that she obeyed her daddy
and her husband
and looked just like her mama
more and more.
that she thought god was
a good idea.
that she cried when she saw
she wasn't beautiful
and tried to be real nice.

■

good times

(1969)

for mama

in the inner city
or
like we call it
home
we think a lot about uptown
and the silent nights
and the houses straight as
dead men
and the pastel lights
and we hang on to our no place
happy to be alive
and in the inner city
or
like we call it
home

■

my mama moved among the days
like a dreamwalker in a field;
seemed like what she touched was hers
seemed like what touched her couldn't hold,
she got us almost through the high grass
then seemed like she turned around and ran
right back in
right back on in

■

my daddy's fingers move among the couplers
chipping steel and skin
and if the steel would break
my daddy's fingers might be men again.

my daddy's fingers wait
grotesque as monkey wrenches
wide and full of angles like the couplers
to chip away the mold's imperfections.

but what do my daddy's fingers
know about grace?
what do the couplers know
about being locked together?

■

lane is the pretty one

her veins run mogen david
and her mind just runs.

the best looking colored girl in town
whose eyes are real light brown
frowns into her glass;

I wish I'd stayed in class.

i wish those lovers
had not looked over
your crooked nose
your too wide mouth

dear sister
dear sister   love

■

miss rosie

when i watch you
wrapped up like garbage
sitting, surrounded by the smell
of too old potato peels
or
when i watch you
in your old man's shoes
with the little toe cut out
sitting, waiting for your mind
like next week's grocery
i say
when i watch you
you wet brown bag of a woman
who used to be the best looking gal in georgia
used to be called the Georgia Rose
i stand up
through your destruction
i stand up

■

robert

was born obedient
without questions

did a dance called
picking grapes
sticking his butt out
for pennies

married a master
who whipped his mind
until he died

until he died
the color of his life
was nigger

■

the 1st

what i remember about that day
is boxes stacked across the walk
and couch springs curling through the air
and drawers and tables balanced on the curb
and us, hollering,
leaping up and around
happy to have a playground;

nothing about the emptied rooms
nothing about the emptied family

■

running across to the lot
in the middle of the cement days
to watch the big boys trembling
as the dice made poets of them
if we remembered to despair
i forget

i forget
while the streetlights were blooming
and the sharp birdcall
of the iceman and his son
and the ointment of the ragman's horse
sang spring
our fathers were dead and
our brothers were dying

■

still
it was nice
when the scissors man come round
running his wheel
rolling his wheel
and the sparks shooting
out in the dark
across the lot
and over to the white folks' section

still
it was nice
in the light of maizie's store
to watch the wheel
and catch the wheel—
fire spinning in the air
and our edges
and our points
sharpening good as anybody's

∎

good times

my daddy has paid the rent
and the insurance man is gone
and the lights is back on
and my uncle brud has hit
for one dollar straight
and they is good times
good times
good times

my mama has made bread
and grampaw has come
and everybody is drunk
and dancing in the kitchen
and singing in the kitchen
oh these is good times
good times
good times

oh children think about the
good times

■

if i stand in my window
naked in my own house
and press my breasts
against my windowpane
like black birds pushing against glass
because i am somebody
in a New Thing

and if the man come to stop me
in my own house
naked in my own window
saying i have offended him
i have offended his

Gods

let him watch my black body
push against my own glass
let him discover self
let him run naked through the streets
crying
praying in tongues

■

stops

they keep coming at me
keep coming at me
all the red lights they got
all the whistles and sirens
blowing with every kind of stop
till i got to go up side a stop
and stop it

even a little old lady
in a liquor store

■

the discoveries of fire

remember
when the skin of your fingers healed
and the smoke rolled away from the
entrance to the cave   how
the rocks cooled down
and you walked back in
once animals and now
men

■

those boys that ran together
at tillman's
and the poolroom
everybody see them now
think it's a shame

everybody see them now
remember they was fine boys

we have some fine black boys

don't it make you want to cry?

■

pity this poor animal
who has never gone beyond
the ape herds gathered around the fires
of europe

all he knows how to do
is huddle with others
in straight haired grunt clusters
to keep warm

and if he has to come out
from the western dirt places
or imitation sun places
and try to make it by himself

he heads, always, for a cave
his mind shivers against the rocks
afraid of the dark
afraid of the cold
afraid to be alone

afraid of the legendary man creature
who is black
and walks on grass
and has no need for fire

■

the white boy

like a man overboard
crying every which way
    is it in your mind
    is it under your clothes
    where oh where is the
    saving thing

■

the meeting after the savior gone
4/4/68

what we decided is
you save your own self.
everybody so quiet.
not so much sorry as
resigned.
we was going to try and save you but
now i guess you got to save yourselves
(even if you don't know
    who you are
    where you been
    where you headed

■

for deLawd

people say they have a hard time
understanding how i
go on about my business
playing my ray charles
hollering at the kids—
seem like my afro
cut off in some old image
would show i got a long memory
and i come from a line
of black and going on women
who got used to making it through murdered sons
and who grief kept on pushing
who fried chicken
ironed
swept off the back steps
who grief kept
for their still alive sons
for their sons coming
for their sons gone
just pushing

∎

ca'line's prayer

i have got old
in a desert country
i am dry
and black as drought
don't make water
only acid
even dogs won't drink

remember me from wydah
remember the child
running across dahomey
black as ripe papaya
juicy as sweet berries
and set me in the rivers of your glory

Ye Ma Jah

■

if he ask you was i laughing

i wonder what become of my mama
and my littlest girl what couldn't run
and i couldn't carry her
and the baby both
and i took him cause he was a man
child
child
pray that the Lord spare hagar
till she explain

■

if something should happen

for instance
if the sea should break
and crash against the decks
and below decks break the cargo
against the sides of the sea
or
if the chains should break
and crash against the decks
and below decks break the sides
of the sea
or
if the seas of cities
should crash against each other
and break the chains
and break the walls holding down the cargo
and break the sides of the seas
and all the waters of the earth wash together
in a rush of breaking
where will the captains run and
to what harbor?

■

generations

people who are going to be
in a few years
bottoms of trees
bear a responsibility to something
besides people
           if it was only
you and me
sharing the consequences
it would be different
it would be just
generations of men
          but
this business of war
these war kinds of things
are erasing those natural
obedient generations
who ignored pride
              stood on no hind legs
              begged no water
              stole no bread
did their own things

and the generations of rice
of coal
of grasshoppers

by their invisibility
denounce us

■

love rejected
hurts so much more
than love rejecting;
they act like they don't love their country
no
what it is
is they found out
their country don't love them.

■

tyrone (1)

on this day
the buffalo soldiers
have taken up position
corner of jefferson and sycamore
we will sack the city
    will sink the city
        seek the city

■

willie b (1)

mama say
i got no business out here
in the army
cause i ain't but twelve
and my daddy was
a white man

the mother fucker

∎

tyrone (2)

the spirit of the buffalo soldiers
is beautiful
how we fight on down to main street
laughing and shouting
we happy together   oh
we turning each other on
in this damn war

■

willie b (2)

why i would bring a wagon into battle
is
a wagon is a help to a soldier
with his bricks
and when he want to rest
also
today is mama's birthday
and i'm gone get her that tv
out of old steinhart's store

■

tyrone (3)

the governor has sent out
jackie robinson
and he has sprinted from center
and crouched low
and caught the ball
(what a shortstop)
and if we buffalo soldiers was sports fans
we sure would cheer

■

willie b (3)

mama say
he was a black hero
a champion like
muhammad ali
but i never heard of it
being not born till 1955

■

tyrone (4)

we made it through the swamps
and we'll make it through the dogs
leaving our white man's names
and white man's traditions
and making some history
and they see the tear gas
burn my buffalo soldiers eyes
they got to say
Look yonder
Tyrone
Is

■

willie b (4)

i'm the one
what burned down the dew drop inn.
yes
the jew do exploit us in his bar
but also
my mama
one time in the dew drop inn
tried for a white man
and if he is on a newspaper
or something
look I am the one what burned down the dew drop inn
everybody say i'm a big boy for my age
me
willie b
son

■

buffalo war

war over
everybody gone home
nobody dead
everybody dying

■

flowers

here we are
running with the weeds
colors exaggerated
pistils wild
embarrassing the calm family flowers   oh
here we are
flourishing for the field
and the name of the place
is Love

■

pork chops
grease stinking out across the field
into the plant where we broke the strike

old man gould sent a train south
picking up niggers
bringing them up no stop
through the polack picket lines
into the plant

chipping like hell
on eight days and off one
sleeping nights between the rows of couplers
hard and stinking out across the field
through the polack picket line
and the strike was broke

lord child i love the union

worked together
slept
fought
in the same town
all the pork chops
fried hard together
stinking together
oh mammy ca'line

a nigger polack ain't shit

■

now my first wife never did come out of her room
until her shoes was buttoned

mama
looked at me and said
you always was a bad boy
and died
gould train come through and
i got on

grampaw's girls was young
could write
their old timey friend was pregnant
and they said they pay my bills
the man was gone
and she was clean as mama

was a girl

never came out of her room
until her shoes was buttoned
scrubbed the wall sometime
twice a day
and i would make her stop   clean
till she died
twenty-one years old

so was grampaw's girl
your mama
i like to marry friends

■

the way it was
working with the polacks
turning into polacks

walked twelve miles into buffalo and
bought a dining room suit

mammy ca'line
walked from new orleans
to virginia
in 1830
seven years old

always said
get what you want
you from dahomey women

first colored man in town
to own a dining room suit
things was changing
new things was coming

you

■

admonitions

boys
i don't promise you nothing
but this
what you pawn
i will redeem
what you steal
i will conceal
my private silence to
your public guilt
is all i got

girls
first time a white man
opens his fly
like a good thing
we'll just laugh
laugh real loud my
black women

children
when they ask you
why is your mama so funny
say
she is a poet
she don't have no sense

■

good news
about the earth

(1972)

for the dead
of jackson and
orangeburg
and so on and
so on and on

about the earth

after kent state

only to keep
his little fear
he kills his cities
and his trees
even his children   oh
people
white ways are
the way of death
come into the
black
and live

■

being property once myself
i have a feeling for it,
that's why i can talk
about environment.
what wants to be a tree,
ought to be he can be it.
same thing for other things.
same thing for men.

■

the way it was

mornings
i got up early
greased my legs
straightened my hair and
walked quietly out
not touching

in the same place
the tree   the lot
the poolroom   deacon moore
everything was stayed

nothing changed
(nothing remained the same)
i walked out quietly
mornings
in the '40s
a nice girl
not touching
trying to be white

■

the lost baby poem

the time i dropped your almost body down
down to meet the waters under the city
and run one with the sewage to the sea
what did i know about waters rushing back
what did i know about drowning
or being drowned

you would have been born in winter
in the year of the disconnected gas
and no car   we would have made the thin
walk over genesee hill into the canada wind
to watch you slip like ice into strangers' hands
you would have fallen naked as snow into winter
if you were here i could tell you these
and some other things

if i am ever less than a mountain
for your definite brothers and sisters
let the rivers pour over my head
let the sea take me for a spiller
of seas   let black men call me stranger
always   for your never named sake

∎

later i'll say
i spent my life
loving a great man

later
my life will accuse me
of various treasons

not black enough
too black
eyes closed when they should have been open
eyes open when they should have been closed

will accuse me for unborn babies
and dead trees

later
when i defend again and again
with this love
my life will keep silent
listening to
my body breaking

■

apology

(to the panthers)

i became a woman
during the old prayers
among the ones who wore
bleaching cream to bed
and all my lessons stayed

i was obedient
but brothers i thank you
for these mannish days

i remember again the wise one
old and telling of suicides
refusing to be slaves

i had forgotten and
brothers i thank you
i praise you
i grieve my whiteful ways

■

lately
everybody i meet
is a poet.

"Look here"

said the tall delivery man
who is always drunk

"whoever can do better
ought to do it. Me,
I'm 25 years old
and all the white boys
my age
are younger than me."

so saying
he dropped a six pack
turned into most of my cousins
and left.

■

the '70s

will be the days
i go unchildrened
strange women will walk
out my door and in
hiding my daughters
holding my sons
leaving me nursing on my self
again
having lost some
begun much

■

listen children
keep this in the place
you have for keeping
always
keep it all ways

we have never hated black

listen
we have been ashamed
hopeless   tired   mad
but always
all ways
we loved us

we have always loved each other
children   all ways

pass it on

■

driving through new england
by broken barns and pastures
i long for the rains of wydah
and the gardens
ripe as history
oranges and citron
limefruit and african apple
not just this springtime and
these wheatfields
white poets call the past.

■

the news

everything changes   the old
songs click like light bulbs
going off   the faces
of men dying scar the air
the moon becomes the mountain
who would have thought
who would believe
dead things could stumble back
and kill us

■

the bodies broken on
the trail of tears
and the bodies melted
in middle passage
are married to rock and
ocean by now
and the mountains crumbling on
white men
the waters pulling white men down
sing for red dust and black clay
good news about the earth

■

song

sons of slaves and
daughters of masters
all come up from the
ocean together

daughters of slaves and
sons of masters
all ride out on the
empty air

brides and hogs and dogs and babies
close their eyes against the sight

bricks and sticks and diamonds witness
a life of death is the death of life

■

prayer

lighten up

why is your hand
so heavy
on just poor
me?

answer

this is the stuff
i made the heroes
out of
all the saints
and prophets and things
had to come by
this

■

heroes

africa

home
oh
home
the soul of your
variety
all of my bones
remember

■

i am high on the man called crazy
who has turned nigger into prince
and broken his words on every ear.
he is blinded by the truth.
his nose is sharp with courage.
this crazy man has given his own teeth
to eat devils and out of mine
he has bitten sons.

■

earth

here is where it was dry
when it rained
and also
here
under the same
what was called
tree
it bore varicolored
flowers   children   bees
all this used to be a
place once   all this
was a nice place
once

■

for the bird who flew against our window one morning and broke his natural neck

my window
is his wall.
in a crash of
birdpride
he breaks the arrogance
of my definitions
and leaves me grounded
in his suicide.

∎

God send easter

and we will lace the
jungle on
and step out
brilliant as birds
against the concrete country
feathers waving as we
dance toward jesus
sun reflecting mango
and apple as we
glory in our skin

■

so close
they come so close
to being beautiful
if they had hung on
maybe five more years
we would have been together
for these new things
and for them old niggers
to have come so close   oh
seem like some black people
missed out even more than
all the time

■

wise: having the ability to perceive and adopt the best means for accomplishing an end.

all the best minds
come into wisdom early.
nothing anybody can say
is profound as
no money   no wine.
all the wise men
on the corner.

■

malcolm

nobody mentioned war
but doors were closed
black women shaved their heads
black men rustled in the alleys like leaves
prophets were ambushed as they spoke
and from their holes black eagles flew
screaming through the streets

■

eldridge

the edge
of this
cleaver
this
straight
sharp
single-
handled
man
will not
rust
break, or
be broken

■

to bobby seale

feel free.
like my daddy
always said
jail wasn't made
for dogs
was made for
men

■

for her hiding place
in whiteness
for angela
straightening her hair
to cloud white eyes
for the yellow skin
of angela
and the scholarships
to hide in
for angela
for angela
if we forget our sister
while they have her
let our hair fall
straight on to our backs
like death

■

richard penniman
when his mama and daddy died
put on an apron and long pants
and raised up twelve brothers and sisters
when a whitey asked one of his brothers one time
is little richard a man (or what?)
he replied in perfect understanding
you bet your faggot ass
he is
you bet your dying ass.

■

daddy
12/02–5/69

the days have kept on coming,
daddy or not.   the cracks
in the sidewalk turn green
and the Indian women sell pussywillows
on the corner.   nothing remembers.
everything remembers.
in the days where daddy was
there is a space.

my daddy died as he lived,
a confident man.
"I'll go to Heaven," he said,
"Jesus knows me."
when his leg died, he cut it off.
"It's gone," he said, "it's gone
but I'm still here."

what will happen to the days
without you
my baby whispers to me.
the days have kept on coming
and daddy's gone.
he knew.
he must have known and
i comfort my son with the hope
the life in the confident man.

■

poem for my sisters

like he always said
        the things of daddy
        will find him
        leg to leg and
        lung to lung
        and the man who
        killed the bear
        so we could cross the mountain
        will cross it whole
        and holy
"all goodby ain't gone"

■

the kind of man he is
for fred

the look of him
the beauty of the man
is in his comings and
his goings from

something is black
in all his instances

he fills
his wife with children and
with things she never knew
so that the sound of him
comes out of her in all directions

his place
is never taken

he is a dark
presence with his friends
and with his enemies
always

which is the thing
which is
the kind of man he is

■

some jesus

adam and eve

the names
of the things
bloom in my mouth

my body opens
into brothers

■

cain

the land of nod
is a desert
on my head   i
plant tears
every morning
my brother
don't rise up

■

moses

i walk on bones
snakes twisting
in my hand
locusts breaking my mouth
an old man
leaving slavery
home is burning in me
like a bush
God got his eye on

■

solomon

i bless the black
skin of the woman
and the black
night turning around her
like a star's bed
and the black
sound of delilah
across his prayers
for they have made me
wise

■

job

job easy
is the pride
of God

job hard
the pride
of job

i come to rags
like a good baby
to breakfast

■

daniel

i have learned
some few things
like when a man
walk manly
he don't stumble
even in the lion's den

■

jonah

what i remember
is green
in the trees
and the leaves
and the smell of mango
and yams
and if i had a drum
i would send to the brothers
—Be care full of the ocean—

■

john

somebody coming in blackness
like a star
and the world be a great bush
on his head
and his eyes be fire
in the city
and his mouth be true as time

he be calling the people brother
even in the prison
even in the jail

i'm just only a baptist preacher
somebody bigger than me coming
in blackness like a star

■

mary

this kiss
as soft as cotton

over my breasts
all shiny bright

something is in this night
oh Lord have mercy on me

i feel a garden
in my mouth

between my legs
i see a tree

■

joseph

something about this boy
has spelled my tongue
so even when my fingers tremble
on mary
my mouth cries only
Jesus   Jesus   Jesus

■

the calling of the disciples

some Jesus
has come on me

i throw down my nets
into water he walks

i loose the fish
he feeds to cities

and everybody calls me
an old name

as i follow out
laughing like God's fool
behind this Jesus

■

the raising of lazarus

the dead shall rise again
whoever say
dust must be dust
don't see the trees
smell rain
remember africa
everything that goes
can come
stand up
even the dead shall rise

■

palm sunday

so here come i
home again
and the people glad
giving thanks
glorying in the brother
laying turnips
for the mule to walk on
waving beets
and collards in the air

■

good friday

i rise up above my self
like a fish flying

men will be gods
if they want it

■

easter sunday

while i was in the middle of the night
I saw red stars and black stars
pushed out of the sky by white ones
and i knew as sure as jungle
is the father of the world
i must slide down like a great dipper of stars
and lift men up

■

spring song

the green of Jesus
is breaking the ground
and the sweet
smell of delicious Jesus
is opening the house and
the dance of Jesus music
has hold of the air and
the world is turning
in the body of Jesus and
the future is possible

■

Uncollected Poems

(1973–1974)

Phillis Wheatley Poetry Festival
November 1973

for Margaret Walker Alexander

I
Hey Nikki
wasn't it good, wasn't it good June
Carole wasn't it good, wasn't it good Alice
Carolyn wasn't it good, Audre wasn't it good
wasn't it good Sonia, sister wasn't it good?

Wasn't it good Margaret, wasn't it good?
Wasn't it good Linda, Mari wasn't it good
wasn't it good Margaret, wasn't it good Naomi
wasn't it good Sarah, sister wasn't it good?

Hey Gloria, Jobari wasn't it good?
Wasn't it good Malaika, wasn't it good?
Wasn't it good sister, wasn't it good sister,
Sister, sisters, sisters, oh sisters,
oh ain't it good?

II
What Nikki knows

Jesus Keep Me is
what kept me and
How I Got Over is
how we got over.

III
to Margaret and Gwen

Mama
two dozen daughters stand together
holding hands and singing cause
you such a good mama we
got to be good girls.

■

All of Us Are All of Us

Malcolm and Martin
George
little Emmett
Billie of the flower
the flower Bessie
all of us are
all of us
Nat
Gabriel
Denmark
Patrice and Kwame
Marcus
black Hampton
all of us are
all of us
Stepen Fetchit
Amos and Andy
Sapphire and
Uncle Tom
all of us are
all of us
Orangeburg
Jackson
Birmingham
here
my Mama
your Daddy
my Daddy
your Mama
oh all of us are
all of us and
this is a poem about
Love

∎

an ordinary woman

(1974)

to fred
you know you know me well

sisters

in salem
to jeanette

weird sister
the black witches know that
the terror is not in the moon
choreographing the dance of wereladies
and the terror is not in the broom
swinging around to the hum of cat music
nor the wild clock face grinning from the wall,
the terror is in the plain pink
at the window
and the hedges moral as fire
and the plain face of the white woman watching us
as she beats her ordinary bread.

■

sisters

for elaine philip on her birthday

me and you be sisters.
we be the same.
me and you
coming from the same place.
me and you
be greasing our legs
touching up our edges.
me and you
be scared of rats
be stepping on roaches.
me and you
come running high down purdy street one time
and mama laugh and shake her head at
me and you.
me and you
got babies
got thirty-five
got black
let our hair go back
be loving ourselves
be loving ourselves
be sisters.
only where you sing
i poet.

■

leanna's poem
for leanna webster

one
is never enough for me
you said
surrounded by the lunch
we could not taste for eating,
and i smiled and thought about meals
and mealmates and hunger
and days and time and life and
hunger, and you are right
it is not, it is never enough;
and so this poem is for us,
leanna, two hungry ladies,
and i wish for you
what i wish for myself—
more than one
more than one
more than one.

■

on the birth of bomani
for jaribu and sababu

we have taken the best leaves
and the best roots
and your mama whose skin
is the color of the sun
has opened into a fire and
your daddy whose skin
is the color of the night
has tended it carefully with
his hunter's hands and
here you have come, bomani,
an afrikan treasure-man.
may the art in the love that made you
fill your fingers,
may the love in the art that made you
fill your heart.

■

salt

for sj and jj

he is as salt
to her,
a strange sweet
a peculiar money
precious and valuable
only to her tribe,
and she is salt
to him,
something that rubs raw
that leaves a tearful taste
but what he will
strain the ocean for and
what he needs.

■

a storm poem
for adrienne

the wind is eating
the world again.
continents spin
on its vigorous tongue
and you adrienne
broken like a bone
should not sink
casual as dinner.
adrienne.
i pronounce your name.
i push your person
into the throat
of this glutton.
for you
let the windmouth burn at last.
for you
let the windteeth break.

■

god's mood

these daughters are bone,
they break.
he wanted stone girls
and boys with branches for arms
that he could lift his life with
and be lifted by.
these sons are bone.

he is tired of years that keep turning into age
and flesh that keeps widening.
he is tired of waiting for his teeth to
bite him and walk away.

he is tired of bone,
it breaks.
he is tired of eve's fancy and
adam's whining ways.

■

new bones

we will wear
new bones again.
we will leave
these rainy days,
break out through
another mouth
into sun and honey time.
worlds buzz over us like bees,
we be splendid in new bones.
other people think they know
how long life is
how strong life is.
we know.

■

harriet
if i be you
let me not forget
to be the pistol
pointed
to be the madwoman
at the rivers edge
warning
be free or die
and isabell
if i be you
let me in my
sojourning
not forget
to ask my brothers
ain't i a woman too
and
grandmother
if i be you
let me not forget to
work hard
trust the Gods
love my children and
wait.

■

roots

call it our craziness even,
call it anything.
it is the life thing in us
that will not let us die.
even in death's hand
we fold the fingers up
and call them greens and
grow on them,
we hum them and make music.
call it our wildness then,
we are lost from the field
of flowers, we become
a field of flowers.
call it our craziness
our wildness
call it our roots,
it is the light in us
it is the light of us
it is the light, call it
whatever you have to,
call it anything.

■

come home from the movies,
black girls and boys,
the picture be over and the screen
be cold as our neighborhood.
come home from the show,
don't be the show.
take off some flowers and plant them,
pick us some papers and read them,
stop making some babies and raise them.
come home from the movies
black girls and boys,
show our fathers how to walk like men,
they already know how to dance.

■

to ms. ann

i will have to forget
your face
when you watched me breaking
in the fields,
missing my children.

i will have to forget
your face
when you watched me carry
your husband's
stagnant water.

i will have to forget
your face
when you handed me
your house
to make a home,

and you never called me sister
then, you never called me sister
and it has only been forever and
i will have to forget your face.

■

my boys
for chan and baggy

my boys beauty is
numberless. no kit
can find their colors
in it. only afrikan artists,
studying forever, can
represent them. they are
brothers to each other
and to other live and
lovely things. people
approaching my boys
in their beauty
stand stunned
questioning over and over—
What is the meaning of this?

■

last note to my girls

for sid, rica, gilly and neen

my girls
my girls
my almost me
mellowed in a brown bag
held tight and straining
at the top
like a good lunch
until the bag turned weak and wet
and burst in our honeymoon rooms.
we wiped the mess and
dressed you in our name and
here you are
my girls
my girls
forty quick fingers
reaching for the door.

i command you to be
good runners
to go with grace
go well in the dark and
make for high ground
my dearest girls
my girls
my more than me.

■

a visit to gettysburg

i will
touch stone
yes i will
teach white rock to answer
yes i will
walk in the wake
of the battle sir
while the hills
and the trees
and the guns watch me
a touchstone
and i will rub
"where is my black blood
and black bone?"
and the grounds
and the graves
will throw off they clothes
and touch stone
for this touchstone.

■

monticello

(history: sally hemmings, slave at monticello,
bore several children with bright red hair)

God declares no independence.
here come sons
from this black sally
branded with jefferson hair.

■

to a dark moses

you are the one
i am lit for.
come with your rod
that twists
and is a serpent.
i am the bush.
i am burning.
i am not consumed.

■

Kali
queen of fatality, she
determines the destiny
of things. nemesis.
the permanent guest
within ourselves.
woman of warfare,
of the chase, bitch
of blood sacrifice and death.
dread mother. the mystery
ever present in us and
outside us. the
terrible hindu woman God
Kali.
who is black.

■

this morning
(for the girls of eastern high school)

this morning
this morning
         i met myself
coming in

a bright
jungle girl
shining
quick as a snake
a tall
tree girl a
me girl
         i met myself
this morning
coming in

and all day
i have been
a black bell
ringing
i survive
         survive
survive

■

i agree with the leaves

the lesson of the falling leaves

the leaves believe
such letting go is love
such love is faith
such faith is grace
such grace is god
i agree with the leaves

■

i am running into a new year
and the old years blow back
like a wind
that i catch in my hair
like strong fingers like
all my old promises and
it will be hard to let go
of what i said to myself
about myself
when i was sixteen and
twentysix and thirtysix
even thirtysix but
i am running into a new year
and i beg what i love and
i leave to forgive me

■

the coming of Kali

it is the black God, Kali,
a woman God and terrible
with her skulls and breasts.
i am one side of your skin,
she sings, softness is the other,
you know you know me well, she sings,
you know you know me well.

running Kali off is hard.
she is persistent with her
black terrible self. she
knows places in my bones
i never sing about but
she knows i know them well.
she knows.
she knows.

■

she insists on me

i offer my
little sister up. no,
she says, no i want
you fat poet with
dead teeth. she insists
on me. my daughters
promise things, they
pretend to be me but
nothing fools her
nothing moves her and
i end up pleading
woman woman i am trying
to make a living here,
woman woman you are not
welcome in these bones,
woman woman please but she
walks past words and
insists on me.

■

she understands me

it is all blood and breaking,
blood and breaking. the thing
drops out of its box squalling
into the light. they are both squalling,
animal and cage. her bars lie wet, open
and empty and she has made herself again
out of flesh out of dictionaries,
she is always emptying and it is all
the same wound the same blood the same breaking.

■

she is dreaming

sometimes
the whole world of women
seems a landscape of
red blood and things
that need healing,
the fears all
fears of the flesh;
will it open
or close
will it scar or
keep bleeding
will it live
will it live
will it live and
will he murder it or
marry it.

■

her love poem

demon, demon, you have dumped me
in the middle of my imagination
and i am dizzy with spinning from
nothing to nothing. it is all your fault
poet, fat man, lover of weak women
and i intend to blame you for it.
i will have you in my head
anyway i can, and it may be love you
or hate you but i will have you
have you have you.

■

calming Kali

be quiet awful woman,
lonely as hell,
and i will comfort you
when i can
and give you my bones
and my blood to feed on.
gently gently now
awful woman,
i know i am your sister.

■

i am not done yet

as possible as yeast
as imminent as bread
a collection of safe habits
a collection of cares
less certain than i seem
more certain than i was
a changed changer
i continue to continue
where i have been
most of my lives is
where i'm going

■

the poet

i beg my bones to be good but
they keep clicking music and
i spin in the center of myself
a foolish frightful woman
moving my skin against the wind and
tap dancing for my life.

■

turning

turning into my own
turning on in
to my own self
at last
turning out of the
white cage, turning out of the
lady cage
turning at last
on a stem like a black fruit
in my own season
at last

■

my poem

a love person
from love people
out of the afrikan sun
under the sign of cancer.
whoever see my
midnight smile
seeing star apple and
mango from home.
whoever take me for
a negative thing,
his death be on him
like a skin
and his skin
be his heart's revenge.

■

lucy one-eye
she got her mama's ways.
big round roller
can't cook
can't clean
if that's what you want
you got it world.

lucy one-eye
she see the world sideways.
word foolish
she say what she don't want
to say, she don't say
what she want to.

lucy one-eye
she won't walk away
from it.
she'll keep on trying
with her crooked look
and her wrinkled ways,
the darling girl.

■

if mama
could see
she would see
lucy sprawling
limbs of lucy
decorating the
backs of chairs
lucy hair
holding the mirrors up
that reflect odd
aspects of lucy.

if mama
could hear
she would hear
lucysong rolled in the
corners like lint
exotic webs of lucysighs
long lucy spiders explaining
to obscure gods.

if mama
could talk
she would talk
good girl
good girl
good girl
clean up your room.

■

i was born in a hotel,
a maskmaker.
my bones were knit by
a perilous knife.
my skin turned around
at midnight and
i entered the earth in
a woman jar.
i learned the world all
wormside up
and this is my yes
my strong fingers;
i was born in a bed of
good lessons
and it has made me
wise.

∎

light
on my mother's tongue
breaks through her soft
extravagant hip
into life.
lucille
she calls the light,
which was the name
of the grandmother
who waited by the crossroads
in virginia
and shot the whiteman off his horse,
killing the killer of sons.
light breaks from her life
to her lives . . .

mine already is
an afrikan name.

■

cutting greens

curling them around
i hold their bodies in obscene embrace
thinking of everything but kinship.
collards and kale
strain against each strange other
away from my kissmaking hand and
the iron bedpot.
the pot is black,
the cutting board is black,
my hand,
and just for a minute
the greens roll black under the knife,
and the kitchen twists dark on its spine
and i taste in my natural appetite
the bond of live things everywhere.

■

jackie robinson

ran against walls
without breaking.
in night games
was not foul
but, brave as a hit
over whitestone fences,
entered the conquering dark.

■

i went to the valley
but i didn't go to stay

i stand on my father's ground
not breaking.
it holds me up
like a hand my father pushes.
virginia.
i am in virginia,
the magic word
rocked in my father's box
like heaven,
the magic line in my hand. but
where is the afrika in this?

except, the grass is green,
is greener he would say.
and the sky opens a better blue
and in the historical museum
where the slaves
are still hidden away like knives
i find a paper with a name i know.
his name.
their name.
sayles.
the name he loved.

i stand on my father's ground
not breaking.
there is an afrikan in this
and whose ever name it has been,
the blood is mine.

my soul got happy
and i stayed all day.

∎

at last we killed the roaches.
mama and me. she sprayed,
i swept the ceiling and they fell
dying onto our shoulders, in our hair
covering us with red. the tribe was broken,
the cooking pots were ours again
and we were glad, such cleanliness was grace
when i was twelve. only for a few nights,
and then not much, my dreams were blood
my hands were blades and it was murder murder
all over the place.

■

in the evenings

i go through my rooms
like a witch watchman
mad as my mother was for
rattling knobs and
tapping glass. ah, lady,
i can see you now,
our personal nurse,
placing the iron
wrapped in rags
near our cold toes.
you are thawed places and
safe walls to me as i walk
the same sentry,
ironing the winters warm and
shaking locks in the night
like a ghost.

■

breaklight

light keeps on breaking.
i keep knowing
the language of other nations.
i keep hearing
tree talk
water words
and i keep knowing what they mean.
and light just keeps on breaking.
last night
the fears of my mother came
knocking and when i
opened the door
they tried to explain themselves
and i understood
everything they said.

■

some dreams hang in the air
like smoke. some dreams
get all in your clothes and
be wearing them more than you do and
you be half the time trying to
hold them and half the time
trying to wave them away.
their smell be all over you and
they get to your eyes and
you cry. the fire be gone
and the wood but some dreams
hang in the air like smoke
touching everything.

■

the carver
for fred

sees the man
in the wood and
calls his name and
the man in the wood
breaks through the bark and
the nations of wood call
the carver
Brother

■

let there be new flowering
in the fields let the fields
turn mellow for the men
let the men keep tender
through the time let the time
be wrested from the war
let the war be won
let love be
at the end

■

the thirty eighth year
of my life,
plain as bread
round as a cake
an ordinary woman.

an ordinary woman.

i had expected to be
smaller than this,
more beautiful,
wiser in afrikan ways,
more confident,
i had expected
more than this.

i will be forty soon.
my mother once was forty.

my mother died at forty four,
a woman of sad countenance
leaving behind a girl
awkward as a stork.
my mother was thick,
her hair was a jungle and
she was very wise
and beautiful
and sad.

i have dreamed dreams
for you mama
more than once.
i have wrapped me
in your skin
and made you live again

more than once.
i have taken the bones you hardened
and built daughters
and they blossom and promise fruit
like afrikan trees.
i am a woman now.
an ordinary woman.

in the thirty eighth
year of my life,
surrounded by life,
a perfect picture of
blackness blessed,
i had not expected this
loneliness.

if it is western,
if it is the final
europe in my mind,
if in the middle of my life
i am turning the final turn
into the shining dark
let me come to it whole
and holy
not afraid
not lonely
out of my mother's life
into my own.
into my own.

i had expected more than this.
i had not expected to be
an ordinary woman.

■

Uncollected Poems

(ca. 1975)

Anniversary

5/10/74

sixteen years
by the white of my hair
by my wide bones
by the life that ran out of me
into life,
sixteen years
and the girl is gone
with her two good eyes;
she was always hoping something,
she was afraid of everything.
little is left of her who hid
behind bread and babies
only something thin and
bright as a flame,
it has no language it can speak
without burning
it has no other house to run to
it loves you loves you loves you.

■

November 1, 1975

My mother is white bones
in a weed field
on her birthday.
She who would be sixty
has been sixteen years
absent at celebrations.
For sixteen years of minutes
she has been what is missing.
This is just to note
the arrogance of days
continuing to happen
as if she were here.

■

"We Do Not Know Very Much About Lucille's Inner Life"

from the light of her inner life
a company of citizens
watches lucille as she trembles
through the world.
she is a tired woman though
well meaning, they say.
when will she learn to listen to us?
lucille things are not what they seem.
all all is wonder and
astonishment.

■

two-headed woman

(1980)

for elaine and eileen
who listen

homage to mine

lucy and her girls

lucy is the ocean
extended by
her girls
are the river
fed by
lucy
is the sun
reflected through
her girls
are the moon
lighted by
lucy
is the history of
her girls
are the place where
lucy
was going

■

i was born with twelve fingers
like my mother and my daughter.
each of us
born wearing strange black gloves
extra baby fingers hanging over the sides of our cribs and
dipping into the milk.
somebody was afraid we would learn to cast spells
and our wonders were cut off
but they didn't understand
the powerful memories of ghosts.   now
we take what we want
with invisible fingers
and we connect
my dead mother   my live daughter   and me
through our terrible shadowy hands.

■

homage to my hair

when i feel her jump up and dance
i hear the music! my God
i'm talking about my nappy hair!
she is a challenge to your hand
black man,
she is as tasty on your tongue as good greens
black man,
she can touch your mind
with her electric fingers and
the grayer she do get, good God,
the blacker she do be!

■

homage to my hips

these hips are big hips
they need space to
move around in.
the don't fit into little
petty places. these hips
are free hips.
they don't like to be held back.
these hips have never been enslaved,
they go where they want to go
they do what they want to do.
these hips are mighty hips.
these hips are magic hips.
i have known them
to put a spell on a man and
spin him like a top!

■

what the mirror said

listen,
you a wonder.
you a city
of a woman.
you got a geography
of your own.
listen,
somebody need a map
to understand you.
somebody need directions
to move around you.
listen,
woman,
you not a noplace
anonymous
girl;
mister with his hands on you
he got his hands on
some
damn
body!

■

there is a girl inside.
she is randy as a wolf.
she will not walk away
and leave these bones
to an old woman.

she is a green tree
in a forest of kindling.
she is a green girl
in a used poet.

she has waited
patient as a nun
for the second coming,
when she can break through gray hairs
into blossom

and her lovers will harvest
honey and thyme
and the woods will be wild
with the damn wonder of it.

■

to merle

say skinny manysided tall on the ball
brown downtown woman
last time i saw you was on the corner of
pyramid and sphinx.
ten thousand years have interrupted our conversation
but I have kept most of my words
till you came back.
what i'm trying to say is
i recognize your language and
let me call you sister, sister,
i been waiting for you.

■

august the 12th
for sam

we are two scars on a dead woman's belly
brother, cut from the same knife
you and me. today is your birthday.
where are you? my hair
is crying for her brother.
myself with a mustache
empties the mirror on our mother's table
and all the phones in august wait.
today is your birthday, call us.
tell us where you are,
tell us why you are silent now.

■

on the death of allen's son

a certain man had seven sons.
who can fill the space that
one space makes?
young friend, young enemy who bloomed
off his stick like a miracle
who will he find to fish the waters
he had saved for you?
his name stood at attention
in seven letters,
now there are six
and it never again
can be pronounced the same.

■

speaking of loss

i began with everything;
parents, two extra fingers
a brother to ruin. i was
a rich girl with no money
in a red dress. how did i come
to sit in this house
wearing a name i never heard
until i was a woman? someone has stolen
my parents and hidden my brother.
my extra fingers are cut away.
i am left with plain hands and
nothing to give you but poems.

■

to thelma who worried because i couldn't cook

because no man would taste you
you tried to feed yourself
kneading your body
with your own fists. the beaten thing
rose up like a dough
and burst in the oven of your hunger.
madam, i'm not your gifted girl,
i am a woman and
i know what to do.

■

poem on my fortieth birthday
to my mother who died young

well i have almost come to the place where you fell
tripping over a wire at the forty-fourth lap
and i have decided to keep running,
head up, body attentive, fingers
aimed like darts at first prize, so
i might not even watch out for the thin thing
grabbing towards my ankles but
i'm trying for the long one mama,
running like hell and if i fall
i fall.

■

february 13, 1980

twenty-one years of my life you have been
the lost color in my eye. my secret blindness,
all my seeings turned gray with your going.
mother, i have worn your name like a shield.
it has torn but protected me all these years,
now even your absence comes of age.
i put on a dress called woman for this day
but i am not grown away from you
whatever i say.

■

forgiving my father

it is friday. we have come
to the paying of the bills.
all week you have stood in my dreams
like a ghost, asking for more time
but today is payday, payday old man;
my mother's hand opens in her early grave
and i hold it out like a good daughter.

there is no more time for you. there will
never be time enough daddy daddy old lecher
old liar. i wish you were rich so i could take it all
and give the lady what she was due
but you were the son of a needy father,
the father of a needy son;
you gave her all you had
which was nothing. you have already given her
all you had.

you are the pocket that was going to open
and come up empty any friday.
you were each other's bad bargain, not mine.
daddy old pauper   old prisoner,   old dead man
what am i doing here collecting?
you lie side by side in debtors' boxes
and no accounting will open them up.

■

to the unborn and waiting children

i went into my mother as
some souls go into a church,
for the rest only. but there,
even there, from the belly of a
poor woman who could not save herself
i was pushed without my permission
into a tangle of birthdays.
listen, eavesdroppers, there is no such thing
as a bed without affliction;
the bodies all may open wide but
you enter at your own risk.

∎

aunt agnes hatcher tells

1. about the war

after the war when rationing was over
was a plenty names. people
shuffled them like cards and drew
new ones out the deck. child,
letters and numbers went
running through whole families.
everybody's cousin was
somebody else. just
consider yourself lucky if
you know who you are.

2. about my mama

your mama, her bottom turned into hamburger
during the war but it was fat meat and
nobody wanted any. she sang Jesus keep me and
beat her fists in fits. fell dead
in the hospital hall
two smiles next to the virgin mary.
glad to be gone.
hunger can kill you.
she's how i know.

3. about my daddy

your daddy, he decided to spread the wealth
as they say, and made another daughter.
just before the war she came calling
looking like his natural blood.
your mama surprised us and opened her heart.
none of his other tricks worked that good.

4. about me

you
slavery time they would be calling you
worth your weight in diamonds the way you
slide out babies like payday from that
billion dollar behind.

■

the once and future dead
who learn they will be white men
weep for their history. we call it
rain.

∎

two-headed woman

in this garden
growing
following strict orders
following the Light
see the sensational
two-headed woman
one face turned outward
one face
swiveling slowly in

■

the making of poems

the reason why i do it
though i fail and fail
in the giving of true names
is i am adam and his mother
and these failures are my job.

■

new year

lucy
by sam
out of thelma
limps down a ramp
toward the rest of her life.
with too many candles
in her hair
she is a princess of
burning buildings
leaving the year that
tried to consume her.
her hands are bright
as they witch for water
and even her tears cry
fire   fire
but she opens herself
to the risk of flame and
walks toward an ocean
of days.

■

sonora desert poem

for lois and richard shelton

1.

the ones who live in the desert,
if you knew them
you would understand everything.
they see it all and
never judge any
just drink the water when
they get the chance.
if i could grow arms on my scars
like them,
if i could learn
the patience they know
i wouldn't apologize for my thorns either
just stand in the desert
and witness.

2. directions for watching the sun set in the desert

come to the landscape that was hidden under the sea.
look in the opposite direction.
reach for the mountain.
the mountain will ignore your hand.
the sun will fall on your back.
the landscape will fade away.
you will think you're alone until a flash
of green incredible light.

3. *directions for leaving the desert*

push the bones back
under your skin.
finish the water.
they will notice your thorns and
ask you to testify.
turn toward the shade.
smile.
say nothing at all.

■

my friends

no they will not understand
when i throw off my legs and my arms
at your hesitant yes.
when i throw them off and slide
like a marvelous snake toward your bed
your box   whatever you will keep me in
no   they will not understand what can be
so valuable beyond paper dollars diamonds
what is to me worth all appendages.
they will never understand   never approve
of me loving at last where i would
throw it all off to be,
with you   in your small room   limbless
but whole.

■

wife

we are some of us
born for the water.
we begin at once
swimming toward him.
we sight him.
we circle him like a ring.
if he does not drown us we stay.
if he does
we swim like a fish for his brother.

■

i once knew a man

i once knew a man who had wild horses killed.
when he told about it
the words came galloping out of his mouth
and shook themselves and headed off in
every damn direction. his tongue
was wild and wide and spinning when he talked
and the people he looked at closed their eyes
and tore the skins off their backs as they walked away
and stopped eating meat.
there was no holding him once he got started;
he had had wild horses killed one time and
they rode him to his grave.

■

angels

"the angels say they have no wings"

two shining women.
i will not betray you with
public naming
nor celebrate actual birthdays.
you are my two good secrets
lady dark   lady fair.
no one will know that I recognize
the rustle of sky in your voices
and your meticulous absence
of wing.

∎

conversation with my grandson, waiting to be conceived

you will bloom
in a family of flowers.
you are the promise
the Light made to adam,
the love you will grow in
is the garden of our lord.

"and i will be a daisy.
daddy too.
mommy is a dandelion. grandma
you are a flower
that has no name."

■

the mystery that surely is present
as the underside of a leaf
turning to stare at you quietly
from your hand,
that is the mystery you have not
looked for, and it turns
with a silent shattering of your life
for who knows ever after
the proper position of things
or what is waiting to turn from us
even now?

■

the astrologer predicts at mary's birth

this one lie down on grass.
this one old men will follow
calling mother   mother.
she womb will blossom then die.
this one she hide from evening.
at a certain time when she hear something
it will burn her ear.
at a certain place when she see something
it will break her eye.

■

anna speaks of the childhood of mary
her daughter

we rise up early and
we work. work is the medicine
for dreams.
            that dream
i am having again;
she washed in light,
whole world bowed to its knees,
she on a hill looking up,
face all long tears.
            and shall i give her up
to dreaming then? i fight this thing.
all day we scrubbing   scrubbing.

■

mary's dream

winged women was saying
"full of grace" and like.
was light beyond sun and words
of a name and a blessing.
winged women to only i.
i joined them, whispering
yes.

■

how he is coming then

like a pot turned on the straw
nuzzled by cows and an old man
dressed like a father. like a loaf
a poor baker sets in the haystack to cool.
like a shepherd who hears in his herding
his mother whisper   my son   my son.

■

holy night

joseph, i afraid of stars,
their brilliant seeing.
so many eyes. such light.
joseph, i cannot still these limbs,
i hands keep moving toward i breasts,
so many stars. so bright.
joseph, is wind burning from east
joseph, i shine, oh joseph,   oh
illuminated night.

■

a song of mary

somewhere it being yesterday.
i a maiden in my mother's house.
the animals silent outside.
is morning.
princes sitting on thrones in the east
studying the incomprehensible heavens.
joseph carving a table somewhere
in another place.
i watching my mother.
i smiling an ordinary smile.

■

island mary

after the all been done and i
one old creature carried on
another creature's back, i wonder
could i have fought these thing?
surrounded by no son of mine save
old men calling mother like in the tale
the astrologer tell, i wonder
could i have walk away when voices
singing in my sleep? i one old woman.
always i seem to worrying now for
another young girl asleep
in the plain evening.
what song around her ear?
what star still choosing?

■

mary   mary astonished by God
on a straw bed circled by beasts
and an old husband. mary marinka
holy woman split by sanctified seed
into mother and mother for ever and ever
we pray for you sister woman shook by the
awe full affection of the saints.

■

for the blind

you will enter morning
without error.
you will stand in a room
where you have never lingered.
you will touch glass.
someone will face you with bones
repeating your bones.
you will feel them in the glass.
your fingers will shine
with recognition,
your eyes will open
with delight.

∎

for the mad

you will be alone at last
in the sanity of your friends.

brilliance will fade away from you
and you will settle in dimmed light.

you will not remember how to mourn
your dying difference.

you will not be better but
they will say you are well.

■

for the lame

happen you will rise,
lift from grounded in a spin
and begin to forget the geography
of fixed things.
happen you will walk past
where you meant to stay,
happen you will wonder at the way
it seemed so marvelous to move.

■

for the mute

they will blow from your mouth one morning
like from a shook bottle
and you will try to keep them for
tomorrow's conversation but
your patience will be broken when the
bottle bursts
and you will spill all of your
extraordinary hearings for there are
too many languages for
one mortal tongue.

■

God waits for the wandering world.
he expects us when we enter,
late or soon.
he will not mind my coming after hours.
his patience is his promise.

■

the light that came to lucille clifton
came in a shift of knowing
when even her fondest sureties
faded away. it was the summer
she understood that she had not understood
and was not mistress even
of her own off eye. then
the man escaped throwing away his tie and
the children grew legs and started walking and
she could see the peril of an
unexamined life.
she closed her eyes, afraid to look for her
authenticity
but the light insists on itself in the world;
a voice from the nondead past started talking,
she closed her ears and it spelled out in her hand
"you might as well answer the door, my child,
  the truth is furiously knocking."

■

the light that came to lucille clifton

testament

in the beginning
was the word.

the year of our lord,
amen. i
lucille clifton
hereby testify
that in that room
there was a light
and in that light
there was a voice
and in that voice
there was a sigh
and in that sigh
there was a world.
a world a sigh a voice a light and
i
alone
in a room.

■

incandescence
formless form
and the soft
shuffle of sound

who are these strangers
peopleing this light?

lucille
we are
the Light

■

mother, i am mad.
we should have guessed
a twelve-fingered flower
might break. my knowing
flutters to the ground.

mother i have managed to unlearn
my lessons. i am left
in otherness. mother

someone calling itself Light
has opened my inside.
i am flooded with brilliance
mother,

someone of it is answering to
your name.

■

perhaps

i am going blind.
my eyes exploding,
seeing more than is there
until they burst into nothing

or going deaf, these sounds
the feathered hum of silence

or going away from my self, the cool
fingers of lace on my skin
the fingers of madness

or perhaps
in the palace of time
our lives are a circular stair
and i am turning

■

explanations

anonymous water can slide under the ground.

the wind can shiver with desire.

this room can settle.

this body can settle.

but can such a sound
cool as a circle
surround and
pray
or promise
or prophesy?

■

friends come

explaining to me that my mind
is the obvious assassin

the terrorist of voices
who has waited
to tell me miraculous lies
all my life. no

i say
friends
the ones who talk to me
their words thin as wire
their chorus fine as crystal
their truth direct as stone,
they are present as air.

they are there.

■

to joan

joan
did you never hear
in the soft rushes of france
merely the whisper of french grass
rubbing against leathern
sounding now like a windsong
now like a man?
did you never wonder
oh fantastical joan,
did you never cry in the sun's face
unreal   unreal? did you never run
villageward
hands pushed out toward your apron?
and just as you knew that your mystery
was broken for all time
did they not fall then
soft as always
into your ear
calling themselves michael
among beloved others?
and you
sister   sister
did you not then sigh
my voices   my voices   of course?

■

confession

father
i am not equal to the faith required.
i doubt.
i have a woman's certainties;
bodies pulled from me,
pushed into me.
bone flesh is what i know.

father
the angels say they have no wings.
i woke one morning
feeling how to see them.
i could discern their shadows
in the shadow. i am not
equal to the faith required.

father
i see your mother standing now
shoulderless and shoeless by your side.
i hear her whisper truths i cannot know.
father i doubt.

father
what are the actual certainties?
your mother speaks of love.

the angels say they have no wings.
i am not equal to the faith required.
i try to run from such surprising presence;
the angels stream before me
like a torch.

■

in populated air
our ancestors continue.
i have seen them.
i have heard
their shimmering voices
singing.

∎

Next

(1987)

*This one or that one dies but never the singer . . . one singer
falls but the next steps into the empty place and sings . . .*

"December Day in Honolulu"
Galway Kinnell

we are all next

album

for lucille chan hall

1 it is 1939.
   our mothers are turning our hair
   around rags.
   our mothers
   have filled our shirley temple cups.
   we drink it all.

2 1939 again.
   our shirley temple curls.
   shirley yellow.
   shirley black.
   our colors are fading.

later we had to learn ourselves
back across 2 oceans
into bound feet and nappy hair.

3 1958 and 9.
   we have dropped daughters,
   afrikan and chinese.
   we think
   they will be beautiful.
   we think
   they will become themselves.

4 it is 1985.
   she is.
   she is.
   they are.

   ∎

winnie song

a dark wind is blowing
the townships into town.
they have burned your house
winnie mandela
but your house has been on fire
a hundred years.
they have locked your husband
in a cage
and it has made him free.
Mandela. Mandala. Mandala
is the universe. the universe
is burning. a dark wind is blowing
the homelands into home.

■

there

there in the homelands
they are arresting children.
they are beating children
and shooting children.
                    in jo'burg
a woman sits on her veranda.
watching her child.
her child is playing on their lawn.
her man comes home from
arresting children. she smiles.
she offers him a drink.
each morning i practice for
getting that woman.
when her sister calls me sister
i remind myself
she is there.

■

what spells raccoon to me
spells more than just his
bandit's eyes
squinting as his furry woman
hunkers down among the fists
of berries.
oh coon
which gave my grandfather a name
and fed his wife on more then one
occasion .
i can no more change my references
than they can theirs.

■

this belief
in the magic of whiteness,
that it is the smooth
pebble in your hand,
that it is the godmother's
best gift,
that it explains,
allows,
assures,
entitles,
that it can sprout singular blossoms
like jack's bean
and singular verandas from which
to watch them rise,
it is a spell
winding round on itself,
grimms' awful fable,
and it turns into capetown and johannesburg
as surely as the beanstalk leads
to the giant's actual country
where jack lies broken at the
meadow's edge
and the land is in ruins,
no magic, no anything.

■

why some people be mad at me sometimes

they ask me to remember
but they want me to remember
their memories
and i keep on remembering
mine.

■

sorrow song

for the eyes of the children,
the last to melt,
the last to vaporize,
for the lingering
eyes of the children, staring,
the eyes of the children of
buchenwald,
of viet nam and johannesburg,
for the eyes of the children
of nagasaki,
for the eyes of the children
of middle passage,
for cherokee eyes, ethiopian eyes,
russian eyes, american eyes,
for all that remains of the children,
their eyes,
staring at us,   amazed to see
the extraordinary evil in
ordinary men.

■

I. at creation

and i and my body rise
with the dusky beasts
with eve and her brother
to gasp in
the insubstantial air
and evenly begin the long
slide out of paradise.
all life is life.
all clay is kin and kin.

∎

I. at gettysburg

if, as they say, this is somehow about myself,
this clash of kin across good farmland, then
why are the ghosts of the brothers and cousins
rising and wailing toward me in their bloody voices,
who are you, nigger woman, who are you?

■

I. at nagasaki

in their own order
the things of my world
glisten into ash. i
have done nothing
to deserve this,
only been to the silver birds
what they have made me.
nothing.

■

I.   at jonestown

on a day when i would have believed
anything, i believed that this white man,
stern as my father, neutral in his coupling
as adam, was possibly who he insisted he was.
now he has brought me to the middle of the
jungle of my life. if i have been wrong, again,
father may even this cup in my hand turn against me.

■

them bones
them bones will
rise again
them bones
them bones will
walk again
them bones
them bones will
talk again
now hear
the word of The Lord
                    —Traditional

atlantic is a sea of bones,
my bones,
my elegant afrikans
connecting whydah and new york,
a bridge of ivory.

seabed they call it.
in its arms my early mothers sleep.
some women leapt with babies in their arms.
some women wept and threw the babies in.

maternal armies pace the atlantic floor.
i call my name into the roar of surf
and something awful answers.

■

cruelty. don't talk to me about cruelty
or what I am capable of.

when i wanted the roaches dead i wanted them dead
and i killed them. i took a broom to their country

and smashed and sliced without warning
without stopping and i smiled all the time i was doing it.

it was a holocaust of roaches, bodies,
parts of bodies, red all over the ground.

i didn't ask their names.
they had no names worth knowing.

now i watch myself whenever i enter a room.
i never know what i might do.

■

the woman in the camp

cbs news
lebanon
1983

they murdered
27 of my family
counting the babies
in the wombs.
some of the men
spilled seed on the ground.
how much is a thousand
thousand?

i had a child.
i taught her to love.
i should have taught her
to fear.
i have learned about blood
and bullets,
where is the love
in my education?

a woman in this camp
has 1 breast and 2 babies.
a woman in this camp
has breasts like mine.
a woman in this camp
watched the stealing
of her husband.
a woman in this camp
has eyes like mine.

alive
i never thought of other women.
if i am ever alive again
i will hold out my female hands.

∎

the lost women

i need to know their names
those women I would have walked with
jauntily the way men go in groups
swinging their arms, and the ones
those sweating women whom I would have joined
after a hard game to chew the fat
what would we have called each other laughing
joking into our beer? where are my gangs,
my teams, my mislaid sisters?
all the women who could have known me,
where in the world are their names?

∎

4 daughters

i am the sieve she strains from
little by little
everyday.

i am the rind
she is discarding.

i am the riddle
she is trying to answer.

something is moving
in the water.
she is the hook.
i am the line.

■

grown daughter

someone is helping me with onions
who peels in the opposite direction
without tears and promises
different soup. i sit with her
watching her   learning to love her but
who is she   who is she   who

■

here is another bone to pick with you
o mother whose bones I worry for scraps,
nobody warned me about daughters;
how they bewitch you into believing
you have thrown off a pot that is yourself
then one night you creep into their rooms and
their faces have hardened into odd flowers
their voices are choosing in foreign elections and
their legs are open to strange unwieldy men.

■

female

there is an amazon in us.
she is the secret we do not
have to learn.
the strength that opens us
beyond ourselves.
birth is our birthright.
we smile our mysterious smile.

■

if our grandchild be a girl

i wish for her
fantastic hands,
twelve spiky fingers
symbols of our tribe.
she will do magic
with them,
she will turn personal
abracadabra
remembered from
dahomean women
wearing
extravagant gloves.

■

this is the tale
i keep on telling
trying to get it right;
the feast of women,
the feeding and
being fed.

■

my dream about being white

hey music and
me
only white,
hair a flutter of
fall leaves
circling my perfect
line of a nose,
no lips,
no behind, hey
white me
and i'm wearing
white history
but there's no future
in those clothes
so i take them off and
wake up
dancing.

■

my dream about the cows

and then i see the cattle of my own town,
rustled already,
prodded by pale cowboys with a foreign smell
into dark pens built to hold them forever,
and then i see a few of them
rib thin and weeping low over
sparse fields and milkless lives but
standing somehow standing,
and then i see how all despair is
thin and weak and personal and
then i see it's only
the dream about the cows.

∎

my dream about time

a woman unlike myself is running
down the long hall of a lifeless house
with too many windows which open on
a world she has no language for,
running and running until she reaches
at last the one and only door
which she pulls open to find each wall
is faced with clocks and as she watches
all of the clocks strike
        NO

■

my dream about falling

a fruitful woman
such as myself
is
falling
notices
she is
an apple
thought
that the blossom
was always
thought
that the tree
was forever
fruitful
a woman
such as
myself.

the fact is the falling.
the dream is the tree.

■

my dream about the second coming

mary is an old woman without shoes.
she doesn't believe it.
not when her belly starts to bubble
and leave the print of a finger where
no man touches.
not when the snow in her hair melts away.
not when the stranger she used to wait for
appears dressed in lights at her
kitchen table.
she is an old woman and
doesn't believe it.

when Something drops onto her toes one night
she calls it a fox
but she feeds it.

■

my dream about God

He is wearing my grandfather's hat.
He is taller than my last uncle.
when He sits to listen
He leans forward tilting the chair

where His chin cups in my father's hand.
it is swollen and hard from creation.
His fingers drum on His knee
dads stern tattoo.

and who do i dream i am
accepting His attentions?

i am the good daughter who stays at home
singing and sewing.
when i whisper He strains to hear me and
He does whatever i say.

■

my dream about the poet

a man.
i think it is a man.
sits down with wood.
i think he's holding wood.
he carves.
he is making a world
he says
as his fingers cut citizens
trees and things
which he perceives to be a world
but someone says that is
only a poem.
he laughs.
i think he is laughing.

■

morning mirror

my mother her sad eyes worn as bark
faces me in the mirror. my mother
whose only sin was dying, whose only
enemy was time, frowns in the glass.
once again she has surprised me
in an echo of her life but
my mother refuses to be reflected;
thelma whose only strength was love,
warns away the glint of likeness,
the woman is loosened in the mirror and
thelma lucille begins her day.

■

or next

the death of crazy horse
9/5/1877
age 35

in the hills where the hoop
of the world
bends to the four directions
WakanTanka has shown me
the path men walk is shadow.

i was a boy when i saw it,
that long hairs and gray beards
and myself
must enter the dream to be real.

so i dreamed and i dreamed
and i endured.

i am the final war chief.
never defeated in battle.
Lakotah, remember my name.

now on this wall my bones
and my heart
are warm in the hands of my father.
WakanTanka has shown me the shadows
will break
near the creek called Wounded Knee.

remember my name, Lakotah.
i am the final war chief.
father, my heart,
never defeated in battle,
father, my bones,
never defeated in battle,
leave them at Wounded Knee

and remember our name. Lakotah.
i am released from shadow.
my horse dreams and dances under me
as i enter the actual world.

■

crazy horse names his daughter

sing the names of the women sing
the power full names of the women sing
White Buffalo Woman who brought the pipe
Black Buffalo Woman and Black Shawl
sing the names of the women sing
the power of name in the women sing
the name i have saved for my daughter sing
her name to the ties and baskets and
the red tailed hawk will take her name and
sing her power to WakanTanka sing
the name of my daughter sing she is
They Are Afraid Of Her.

■

crazy horse instructs the young men but in their grief they forget

cousins if i be betrayed
paint my body red and
plunge it in fresh water.
i will be restored. if not
my bones will turn to stone
my joints to flint and my spirit
will watch and wait.

it is more than one hundred years.
grandmother earth rolls her shoulders
in despair. her valleys are flooded
fresh with water and blood.
surely the heart of crazy horse must rise
and rebone itself.
to me my tribes.
to me my horses.
to me my medicine.

■

the message of crazy horse

i would sit in the center of the world,
the Black Hills hooped around me and
dream of my dancing horse. my wife

was Black Shawl who gave me the daughter
i called They Are Afraid Of Her.
i was afraid of nothing

except Black Buffalo Woman.
my love for her i wore
instead of feathers. i did not dance

i dreamed. i am dreaming now
across the worlds. my medicine is strong.
my medicine is strong in the Black basket
of these fingers. i come through this

Black Buffalo woman. hear me;
the hoop of the world is breaking.
fire burns in the four directions.
the dreamers are running away from the hills.
i have seen it. i am crazy horse.

∎

the death of thelma sayles
2/13/59
age 44

i leave no tracks so my live loves
can't follow. at the river
most turn back, their souls shivering,
but my little girl stands alone on the bank
and watches. i pull my heart out of my pocket
and throw it. i smile as she catches all
she'll ever catch and heads for home
and her children. mothering
has made it strong, i whisper in her ear
along the leaves.

■

lives

to lu in answer to her question

you have been a fisherman,
simple and poor. you
struggled all your days and
even at the end you fought
and did not win. your son
was swimming. fearing
for his life you
rushed toward him. and drowned.

once a doctor, bitter,
born in a cold climate,
you turned your scalpel
on the world and cut your way
to the hangman.

humans who speak of royal lives
amuse Them. you have heard of course
of the splendid court of sheba;
you were then. you were not there.

■

the message of thelma sayles

baby, my only husband turned away.
for twenty years my door was open.
nobody ever came.

the first fit broke my bed.
i woke from ecstasy to ask
what blood is this? am i the bride of Christ?
my bitten tongue was swollen for three days.

i thrashed and rolled from fit to death.
you are my only daughter.

when you lie awake in the evenings
counting your birthdays
turn the blood that clots your tongue
into poems. poems.

■

the death of joanne c.

11/30/82
aged 21

i am the battleground that
shrieks like a girl.
to myself i call myself
gettysburg. laughing,
twisting the i.v.,
laughing or crying, i can't tell
which anymore,
i host the furious battling of
a suicidal body and
a murderous cure.

■

enter my mother
wearing a peaked hat.
her cape billows,
her broom sweeps the nurses away,
she is flying, the witch of the ward, my mother
pulls me up by the scruff of the spine
incanting   Live   Live   Live!

■

leukemia as white rabbit

running always running murmuring
she will be furious   she will be
furious, following a great
cabbage of a watch that tells only
terminal time, down deep into a
rabbit hole of diagnosticians shouting
off with her hair   off with her skin and
i am   i am   i am   furious.

■

incantation
overheard in hospital

pluck the hairs
from the head
of a virgin.
sweep them into the hall.
take a needle
thin as a lash,
puncture the doorway
to her blood.
here is the magic word:
cancer.
cancer.
repeat it, she will
become her own ghost.
repeat it, she will
follow you, she will
do whatever you say.

■

chemotherapy

my hair is pain.
my mouth is a cave of cries.
my room is filled with white coats
shaped like God.
they are moving their fingers along
their stethoscopes.
they are testing their chemical faith.
chemicals   chemicals   oh mother mary
where is your living child?

■

she won't ever forgive me,
the willful woman,
for not becoming a pine box
of wrinkled dust according to plan.
i can hear her repeating my dates:
1962 to 1982 or 3. mother
forgive me, mother believe
i am trying to make old bones.

■

the one in the next bed is dying.
mother we are all next. or next.

■

leukemia as dream/ritual

it is night in my room.
the woman beside me is dying.
a small girl stands
at the foot of my bed.
she is crying and carrying wine
and a wafer.
her name is the name i would have given
the daughter i would have liked to have had.
she grieves for herself and
not for the woman.
she mourns the future and
not the past.
she offers me her small communion.
i roll the wafer and wine on my tongue.
i accept my body. i accept my blood.
eat she whispers. drink and eat.

■

the message of jo

my body is a war
nobody is winning.
my birthdays are tired.
my blood is a white flag,
waving.
surrender,
my darling mother,
death is life.

■

chorus: lucille

something is growing in the strong man.
it is blooming, they say, but not a flower.
he has planted so much in me. so much.
i am not willing, gardener, to give you up to this.

■

the death of fred clifton

11/10/84
age 49

i seemed to be drawn
to the center of myself
leaving the edges of me
in the hands of my wife
and i saw with the most amazing
clarity
so that i had not eyes but
sight,
and, rising and turning
through my skin,
there was all around not the
shapes of things
but oh, at last, the things
themselves.

∎

"i'm going back to my true identity"
fjc 11/84

i was ready to return
to my rightful name.
i saw it hovering near
in blazoned script
and, passing through fire,
i claimed it. here
is a box of stars
for my living wife.
tell her to scatter them
pronouncing no name.
tell her there is no deathless name
a body can pronounce.

■

my wife

wakes up, having forgotten.
my closet door gapes wide,
an idiot mouth, and inside
all of the teeth are missing.
she closes her eyes and weeps
toward my space in the bed, "Darling,
something has stolen your wonderful
shirts and ties."

■

the message of fred clifton

i rise up from the dead before you
a nimbus of dark light
to say that the only mercy
is memory,
to say that the only hell
is regret.

■

singing

one singer falls but the next steps into the empty place
and sings . . .

"December Day in Honolulu"
Galway Kinnell

in white america

1   i come to read them poems

i come to read them poems,
a fancy trick i do
like juggling with balls of light.
i stand, a dark spinner,
in the grange hall,
in the library, in the
smaller conference room,
and toss and catch as if by magic,
my eyes bright, my mouth smiling,
my singed hands burning.

2   the history

1800's in this town
fourteen longhouses were destroyed
by not these people here.
not these people
burned the crops and chopped down
all the peach trees.
not these people. these people
preserve peaches, even now.

3   the tour

"this was a female school.
my mother's mother graduated
second in her class.
they were taught embroidery,
and chenille and filigree,
ladies' learning. yes,

we have a liberal history here."
smiling she pats my darky hand.

4   the hall

in this hall
dark women
scrubbed the aisles
between the pews
on their knees.
they could not rise
to worship.
in this hall
dark women
my sisters and mothers

though i speak with the tongues
of men and of angels and
have not charity . . .

in this hall
dark women,
my sisters and mothers,
i stand
and let the church say
let the church say
let the church say
AMEN.

5   the reading

i look into none of my faces
and do the best i can.
the human hair between us
stretches but does not break.

i slide myself along it and
love them, love them all.

6   *it is late*

it is late
in white america.
i stand
in the light of the
7-11
looking out toward
the church
and for a moment only
i feel the reverberation
of myself
in white america
a black cat
in the belfry
hanging
and
ringing.

■

shapeshifter poems

1

the legend is whispered
in the women's tent
how the moon when she rises
full
follows some men into themselves
and changes them there
the season is short
but dreadful   shapeshifters
they wear strange hands
they walk through the houses
at night   their daughters
do not know them

2

who is there to protect her
from the hands of the father
not the windows which see and
say nothing   not the moon
that awful eye   not the woman
she will become with her
scarred tongue   who   who   who   the owl
laments into the evening   who
will protect her   this   prettylittlegirl

3

if the little girl lies
still enough
shut enough

hard enough
shapeshifter may not
walk tonight
the full moon may not
find him here
the hair on him
bristling
rising
up

4

the poem at the end of the world
is the poem the little girl breathes
into her pillow   the one
she cannot tell   the one
there is no one to hear   this poem
is a political poem   is a war poem   is a
universal poem but is not about
these things   this poem
is about one human heart   this poem
is the poem at the end of the world

■

california lessons

1 *geography*

over there is asia
watching from the water
astounded as siddhartha.
over there, asia,
waiting in the water
for what is surely turning
on the wheel. here
is california
swinging from the edge
of the darkening of america
and over there, sitting,
patient as gautama
enlightened, in the water,
is asia.

2 *history*

guard your language

what bird remembers
the songs
the miwok sang?

guard your life

pomo
shasta
esalen

peoples
not places

3 *botany*

"all common figs
can produce fertile seeds
if the flowers
are pollinated."

in concord
in 1985
a black man
was hung
from a fig tree.

"the fruit
is dark
and sweet."

4 *semantics*

in 1942
almost all
the japanese
were concentrated
into camps.
intern ment
but no doctor came.

5 *metaphysics*

question: what is karma?

answer: there is a wheel
             and it is turning.

■

quilting

poems 1987–1990

for maude meehan
homegirl

quilting

somewhere in the unknown world
a yellow eyed woman
sits with her daughter
quilting.

some other where
alchemists mumble over pots.
their chemistry stirs
into science. their science
freezes into stone.

in the unknown world
the woman
threading together her need
and her needle
nods toward the smiling girl
remember
this will keep us warm.

how does this poem end?
    do the daughters' daughters quilt?
    do the alchemists practice their tables?
    do the worlds continue spinning
    away from each other forever?

■

log cabin

i am accused of tending to the past
as if i made it,
as if i sculpted it
with my own hands. i did not.
this past was waiting for me
when i came,
a monstrous unnamed baby,
and i with my mother's itch
took it to breast
and named it
History.
she is more human now,
learning language everyday,
remembering faces, names and dates.
when she is strong enough to travel
on her own, beware, she will.

■

note to myself

it's a black thing you wouldn't understand
$\qquad\qquad\qquad\qquad$ *(t-shirt)*

amira baraka—*i refuse to be judged by white men.*

or defined. and i see
that even the best believe
they have that right,
believe that
what they say i mean
is what i mean
as if words only matter in the world they know,
as if when i choose words
i must choose those
that they can live with
even if something inside me
cannot live,
as if my story is
so trivial
we can forget together,
as if i am not scarred,
as if my family enemy
does not look like them,
as if i have not reached
across our history to touch,
to soothe on more than one
occasion
and will again,
although the merely human
is denied me still
and i am now no longer beast
but saint.

■

poem beginning in no and ending in yes

for hector peterson, age 13
first child killed in soweto riot, 1976

no
light there was no light at first around the head
of the young boy   only the slim stirring of soweto
only the shadow of voices   students and soldiers
practicing their lessons   and one and one cannot be even
two in afrikaans   then before the final hush
in the schoolyard in soweto   there was the burning of his name
into the most amazing science   the most ancient prophesy
let there be light and there was light around the young
boy hector peterson dead in soweto and still among us
yes

■

february 11, 1990

for Nelson Mandela and Winnie

nothing so certain as justice.
nothing so certain as time.
so he would wait seven days, or years
or twenty-seven even,
firm in his certainty.
nothing so patient as truth.
nothing so faithful as now.
walk out old chief, old husband,
enter again your own wife.

■

at the cemetery, walnut grove plantation, south carolina, 1989

among the rocks
at walnut grove
your silence drumming
in my bones,
tell me your names.

nobody mentioned slaves
and yet the curious tools
shine with your fingerprints.
nobody mentioned slaves
but somebody did this work
who had no guide, no stone,
who moulders under rock.

tell me your names,
tell me your bashful names
and i will testify.

the inventory lists ten slaves
but only men were recognized.

among the rocks
at walnut grove
some of these honored dead
were dark
some of these dark
were slaves
some of these slaves
were women
some of them did this
honored work.
tell me your names
foremothers, brothers,

tell me your dishonored names.
here lies
here lies
here lies
here lies
hear

∎

slave cabin, sotterly plantation, maryland, 1989

in this little room
note carefully

aunt nanny's bench

three words that label
things
aunt
is my parent's sister
nanny
my grandmother
bench
the board at which
i stare
the soft curved polished
wood
that held her bottom
after the long days
without end
without beginning
when she   aunt nanny   sat
feet dead against the dirty floor
humming for herself   humming
her own sweet human name

■

white lady

a street name for cocaine

wants my son
wants my niece
wants josie's daughter
holds them hard
and close as slavery
what will it cost
to keep our children
what will it cost
to buy them back.

white lady
says i want you
whispers
let me be your lover
whispers
run me through your
fingers
feel me smell me taste me
love me
nobody understands you like
white lady

white lady
you have chained our sons
in the basement
of the big house
white lady

you have walked our daughters
out into the streets
white lady
what do we have to pay

to repossess our children
white lady
what do we have to owe
to own our own at last

■

memo

to fannie lou hamer

fannie for this
you never walked
miles through the mud
to register the vote
not for this
fannie did you stand
a wall in the hall
of justice not for these
stoned girls and boys
were you a brick
building a mississippi
building freedom
into a party not
this party fannie
where they lie eyes
cold and round as death
doing to us what even
slavery couldn't

■

[from a letter written to Dr. W. E. B. Dubois by Alvin Borgquest of Clark University in Massachusetts and dated April 3, 1905:

"We are pursuing an investigation here on the subject of crying as an expression of the emotions, and should like very much to learn about its peculiarities among the colored people. We have been referred to you as a person competent to give us information on the subject. We desire especially to know about the following salient aspects: 1. Whether the Negro sheds tears. . . ."]

reply

he do
she do
they live
they love
they try
they tire
they flee
they fight
they bleed
they break
they moan
they mourn
they weep
they die
they do
they do
they do

■

whose side are you on?

the side of the busstop woman
trying to drag her bag
up the front steps before the doors
clang shut   i am on her side
i give her exact change
and him the old man hanging by
one strap his work hand folded shut
as the bus doors i am on his side
when he needs to leave
i ring the bell   i am on their side
riding the late bus into the same
someplace   i am on the dark side always
the side of my daughters
the side of my tired sons

■

shooting star

who would i expect
to understand
what it be like
what it be like
living under a star
that hates you. you
spend a half life
looking for your own
particular heaven,
expecting to be found
one day on a sidewalk
in a bad neighborhood,
face toward the sky,
hoping some body saw
a blaze of light perhaps
a shooting star
some thing to make it mean
some thing.   yo,
that brilliance there,
is it you, huey?
is it huey?
is it you?

> *for huey p. newton*
> *r.i.p.*

■

poem with rhyme in it

black people we live in the land
of ones who have cut off their own
two hands
and cannot pick up the strings
connecting them to their lives
who cannot touch   whose things
have turned into planets more dangerous
than mars
but i have listened this long dark night
to the stars
black people and though the ground
be bitter as salt
they say it is not our fault

■

eyes

for Clarence Fountain and the Five Blind Boys Of Alabama
after viewing THE GOSPEL AT COLONUS, the story of
Oedipus transplanted to a Southern Baptist Church, and
thinking of my grandfather and the history of my people
on this land. Each section opens with lyrics quoted from
the musical.

> "Here they are. The soft eyes open."
> —James Dickey

1.
live where you can
be happy as you can
happier than god has made your father

wandering colonus
as you have wandered selma
and montgomery
as you have circuited
the southern church halls
half-emptied by a young war
wandered from your mothers
then seeking them again   again
the dim remembered breasts
offered without judgement
live
you sing to us
live where you can

2.
where have we come to now
what ground is this
what god is honored here

the fields of alabama sparkle in the sun   on
broadway
five old men
sparkle in white suits
their fingers light
on one another's back   lights
proclaim The Five Blind Boys
Of Alabama   five old men
black and blind
who have no names save one
what ground is this
what god

3.
i could say much to you
if you could understand me

the gods announce themselves to men
by name   clarence fountain's hand
pushes aside the air
between himself and vision
vision of resting place
of sanctuary
clarence fountain's hand
commands the air
he has seen what he has seen
it has been enough

4.
a voice foretold
that i shall find
sanctuary

somewhere in alabama
a baby is born to a girl
in a tarpaper room
his blind hand shivers
groping toward her breasts
as toward a lamp
she holds him to her
and begins to sing
live where you can
be happy as you can
slowly
the soft eyes open

5.
all eyes fail
before time's eye

it has been enough
slowly the soft eyes open
what ground is this
what god
i could say much to you
be happy as you can

■

defending my tongue

what i be talking about
can be said in this language
only   this tongue
be the one that understands
what i be talking about

you are you talking about
the landscape that would break me
if it could   the trees
my grandfolk swung from   the dirt
they planted in and ate

no what i be talking about
the dirt   the tree   the land
scape can only be said
in this language   the words
be hard be bumping out too much
to be contained in one thin tongue
like this language   this landscape   this life

■

catalpa flower

from the wisdom of sister brown

1.
on sisterhood

some of our sisters
who put down the bucket
lookin for us
to pick it up

2.
on lena (born 6/30/17)

people talk about beautiful
and look at lizabeth taylor
lena just stand there smilin
a tricky smile

3.
on the difference between
eddie murphy and richard pryor

eddie, he a young blood
he see somethin funny
in everythin   ol rich
been around a long time
he know aint nothin
really funny

■

the birth of language

and adam rose
fearful in the garden
without words
for the grass
his fingers plucked
without a tongue
to name the taste
shimmering in his mouth
did they draw blood
the blades   did it become
his early lunge
toward language
did his astonishment
surround him
did he shudder
did he whisper
eve

■

we are running

running and
time is clocking us
from the edge like an only
daughter.
our mothers stream before us,
cradling their breasts in their
hands.
oh pray that what we want
is worth this running,
pray that what we're running
toward
is what we want.

■

what the grass knew

after some days, toward evening,
He stood under a brackish sky
trembling and blaming creation.
but the grass knew that what is built
is finally built for others,
that firmament is not enough, that
tiger was coming and partridge and
whale and even their raucous voices
would not satisfy. He, walking
the cool of the garden, lonely
as light, realized that He must feed
His own hunger or die. adam,
He nodded, adam,
while the understanding grass
prepared itself for eve.

■

nude photograph

here is the woman's
soft and vulnerable body,
every where on her turning
round into another
where. shadows on her
promising mysterious places
promising the answers to
questions impossible to ask.
who could rest one hand here or here
and not feel, whatever the shape
of the great hump longed for
in the night, a certain joy, a certain,
yes, satisfaction, yes.

■

this is for the mice that live
behind the baseboard,
she whispered, her fingers
thick with cheese. what i do
is call them, copying their own
voices; please please please
sweet please. i promise
them nothing. they come
bringing nothing and we sit
together, nuzzling each other's
hungry hands. everything i want
i have to ask for, she sighed.

■

sleeping beauty

when she woke up
she was terrible.
under his mouth her mouth
turned red and warm
then almost crimson as the coals
smothered and forgotten
in the grate.
she has been gone so long.
there was so much to unlearn.
she opened her eyes.
he was the first thing she saw
and she blamed him.

∎

a woman who loves
impossible men
sits a long time indoors
watching her windows
she has no brother
who understands
where she is not going
her sisters offer their
own breasts up, full and
creamy vessels but she
cannot drink because
she loves impossible men

a woman who loves
impossible men
listens at night to music
she cannot sing
she drinks good sherry
swallowing around the notes
rusted in her throat
but she does not fill
she is already full
of love for impossible men

a woman who loves
impossible men
promises each morning
that she will take this day in her
hands
disrobe it   lie with it
learn to love it
but she doesn't   she walks by
strangers   walks by kin
forgets their birthmarks

their birthdays
remembers only the names
the stains of impossible men

∎

man and wife

she blames him, at the last, for
backing away from his bones
and his woman, from the life
he promised her was worth
cold sheets. she blames him
for being unable to see
the tears in her eyes, the birds
hovered by the window, for love being
not enough, for leaving.

he blames her, at the last, for
holding him back with her eyes
beyond when the pain was more
than he was prepared to bear,
for the tears he could neither
end nor ignore, for believing
that love could be enough,
for the birds, for the life
so difficult to leave.

■

poem in praise of menstruation

if there is a river
more beautiful than this
bright as the blood
red edge of the moon   if

there is a river
more faithful than this
returning each month
to the same delta   if there

is a river
braver than this
coming and coming in a surge
of passion, of pain   if there is

a river
more ancient than this
daughter of eve
mother of cain and of abel   if there is in

the universe such a river   if
there is some where water
more powerful than this wild
water
pray that it flows also
through animals
beautiful and faithful and ancient
and female and brave

■

peeping tom

sometimes at night he dreams back
thirty years
to the alley outside our room
where he stands, a tiptoed boy
watching the marvelous thing
a man turning into a woman.
sometimes
beating himself with his own fist
into that spilled boy and the
imagined world of that man
that woman that night, he lies
turned from his natural wife.
sometimes he searches the window for
a plaid cap, two wide eyes.

■

ways you are not like oedipus

for Michael Glaser

you have spared your father
you pass the sphinx without
answering   you recognized
your mother in time
your sons covet only
their own kingdoms
you lead your daughters
even in your blindness
you do not wander far
from your own good house
it is home and you know it

■

the killing of the trees

the third went down
with a sound almost like flaking,
a soft swish as the left leaves
fluttered themselves and died.
three of them, four, then five
stiffening in the snow
as if this hill were Wounded Knee
as if the slim feathered branches
were bonnets of war
as if the pale man seated
high in the bulldozer nest
his blonde mustache ice-matted
was Pahuska come again but stronger now,
his long hair wild and unrelenting.

remember the photograph,
the old warrior, his stiffened arm
raised as if in blessing,
his frozen eyes open,
his bark skin brown and not so much
wrinkled as circled with age,
and the snow everywhere still falling,
covering his one good leg.
remember his name was Spotted Tail
or Hump or Red Cloud or Geronimo
or none of these or all of these.
he was a chief. he was a tree
falling the way a chief falls,
straight, eyes open, arms reaching
for his mother ground.

so i have come to live
among the men who kill the trees,
a subdivision, new,

in southern Maryland.
I have brought my witness eye with me
and my two wild hands,
the left one sister to the fists
pushing the bulldozer against the old oak,
the angry right, brown and hard and spotted
as bark. we come in peace,
but this morning
ponies circle what is left of life
and whales and continents and children and ozone
and trees huddle in a camp weeping
outside my window and i can see it all
with that one good eye.

■

pahuska=long hair, lakota name for custer

questions and answers

what must it be like
to stand so firm, so sure?

in the desert even the saguro
hold on as long as they can

twisting their arms in
protest or celebration.

you are like me,
understanding the surprise

of jesus, his rough feet
planted on the water

the water lapping
his toes and holding them.

you are like me, like him
perhaps, certain only that

the surest failure
is the unattempted walk.

■

november 21, 1988

25 years

those days
before the brain blew back
mottled and rusting against the pink coat
them days
when the word had meaning
as well as definition
those days
when honor was honorable and
good and right were good and right
them days
when the spirit of hope
reached toward us waving a wide hand
and smiling toward us   yes
those days
them days
the days
before the bubble closed
over the top of the world   no
this is not better than that

■

the beginning of the end of the world

cockroach population possibly declining
                              —news report

maybe the morning the roaches
walked into the kitchen
bold with they bad selves
marching up out of the drains
not like soldiers   like priests
grim and patient in the sink
and when we ran the water
trying to drown them as if they were
soldiers   they seemed to bow their
sad heads   for us not at us
and march single file away

maybe then   the morning we rose
from our beds as always
listening for the bang of the end
of the world   maybe then
when we heard only the tiny tapping
and saw them dark and prayerful
in the kitchen   maybe then
when we watched them turn from us
faithless at last
and walk in a long line away

■

the last day

we will find ourselves surrounded
by our kind   all of them now
wearing the eyes they had
only imagined possible
and they will reproach us
with those eyes
in a language more actual
than speech
asking why we allowed this
to happen   asking why
for the love of God
we did this to ourselves
and we will answer
in our feeble voices   because
because   because

■

eight-pointed star

wild blessings

licked in the palm of my hand
by an uninvited woman. so i have held
in that hand the hand of a man who
emptied into his daughter, the hand
of a girl who threw herself
from a tenement window, the trembling
junkie hand of a priest, of a boy who
shattered across viet nam
someone resembling his mother,
and more. and more.
do not ask me to thank the tongue
that circled my fingers
or pride myself on the attentions
of the holy lost.
i am grateful for many blessings
but the gift of understanding,
the wild one, maybe not.

■

somewhere
some woman
just like me
tests the lock on the window
in the children's room,
lays out tomorrow's school clothes,
sets the table for breakfast early,
finds a pen between the cushions
on the couch
sits down and writes the words
Good Times.
i think of her as i begin to teach
the lives of the poets,
about her space at the table
and my own inexplicable life.

■

1

when i stand around among poets
i am embarrassed mostly,
their long white heads,
the great bulge in their pants,

their certainties.

i don't know how to do
what i do in the way
that i do it. it happens
despite me and i pretend

to deserve it.

but i don't know how to do it.
only sometimes when
something is singing
i listen and so far

i hear.

2

when i stand around
among poets, sometimes
i hear a single music
in us, one note
dancing us through the
singular moving world.

■

water sign woman

the woman who feels everything
sits in her new house
waiting for someone to come
who knows how to carry water
without spilling, who knows
why the desert is sprinkled
with salt, why tomorrow
is such a long and ominous word.

they say to the feel things woman
that little she dreams is possible,
that there is only so much
joy to go around, only so much
water. there are no questions
for this, no arguments. she has

to forget to remember the edge
of the sea, they say, to forget
how to swim to the edge, she has
to forget how to feel. the woman
who feels everything sits in her
new house retaining the secret
the desert knew when it walked
up from the ocean, the desert,

so beautiful in her eyes;
water will come again
if you can wait for it.
she feels what the desert feels.
she waits.

■

photograph

my grandsons
spinning in their joy

universe
keep them turning   turning
black blurs against the window
of the world
for they are beautiful
and there is trouble coming
round and round and round

■

grandma, we are poets

for anpeyo brown

autism: from the Webster's New Universal Dictionary
      and the Random House Encyclopedia

in psychology a state of mind
characterized by daydreaming

say rather
i imagined myself
in the place before
language imprisoned itself
in words

by failure to use language normally

say rather that labels
and names rearranged themselves
into description
so that what i saw
i wanted to say

by hallucinations, and ritualistic and repetitive
patterns of behavior
such as excessive rocking and spinning

say rather circling and
circling my mind i am sure i imagined
children without small rooms
imagined young men black and
filled with holes imagined
girls imagined old men penned
imagine actual humans
howling their animal fear

by failure to relate to others

say rather they began
to recede to run back
ward as it were
into a world of words
apartheid   hunger   war
i could not follow

by disregard of external reality,
withdrawing into a private world

say rather i withdrew
to seek within myself
some small reassurance
that tragedy while vast
is bearable

■

december 7, 1989

this morning your grandmother
sits in the shadow of
Pearl drinking her coffee.
a sneak attack would find me
where my mother sat that day,
flush against her kitchen table,
her big breasts leaning into
the sugar spill. and it is sweet
to be here in the space between
one horror and another
thinking that history
happens all the time
but is remembered backward
in labels not paragraphs.
and so i claim this day
and offer it
this paragraph i own
to you, peyo, dakotah,
for when you need some
memory, some honey thing
to taste, and call the past.

■

to my friend, jerina

listen,
when i found there was no safety
in my father's house
i knew there was none anywhere.
you are right about this,
how i nurtured my work
not my self, how i left the girl
wallowing in her own shame
and took on the flesh of my mother.
but listen,
the girl is rising in me,
not willing to be left to
the silent fingers in the dark,
and you are right,
she is asking for more than
most men are able to give,
but she means to have what she
has earned,
sweet sighs, safe houses,
hands she can trust.

■

lot's wife   1988

each of these weeds is a day
i climbed the stair
at 254 purdy street
and looked into a mirror
to see if i was really there.
i was there.   i am there
in the thousand days.
the weeds.   and these weeds

were 11 harwood place
that daddy bought expecting it
to hold our name forever
against the spin of the world.

our name is spinning away in the wind
blowing across the vacant lots
of buffalo, new york,
that were my girlhood homes.

sayles, i hear them calling, sayles,
we thought we would live forever;
and i look back like lot's wife
wedded to her weeds and turn to something
surer than salt and write this, yes
i promise, yes we will.

■

fat fat
water rat

imagine the children singing
to a thin woman. imagine
her tight lips, the shadow
and bone of her ass
as she enters this room
and you see her and whisper,
beautiful.

imagine she is myself,
next year perhaps, passing
the now silent children,
entering this room and you,
not recognizing the water rat,
feel your tongue thickening,
everything thickening.

in my dream i swim away from her
as often as toward. in my dream
the children are singing
or silent, it never matters,
and i am of uncertain size
and shape, lying splendid in
a giant's bed. imagine this room
and me spreading for you my thighs,
my other beautiful things.

■

poem to my uterus

you   uterus
you have been patient
as a sock
while i have slippered into you
my dead and living children
now
they want to cut you out
stocking i will not need
where i am going
where am i going
old girl
without you
uterus
my bloody print
my estrogen kitchen
my black bag of desire
where can i go
barefoot
without you
where can you go
without me

■

to my last period

well girl, goodbye,
after thirty-eight years.
thirty-eight years and you
never arrived
splendid in your red dress
without trouble for me
somewhere, somehow

now it is done
and i feel just like
the grandmothers who,
after the hussy has gone,
sit holding her photograph
and sighing, *wasn't she
beautiful? wasn't she beautiful?*

■

wishes for sons

i wish them cramps.
i wish them a strange town
and the last tampon.
i wish them no 7-11.

i wish them one week early
and wearing a white skirt.
i wish them one week late.

later i wish them hot flashes
and clots like you
wouldn't believe.   let the
flashes come when they
meet someone special.
let the clots come
when they want to.

let them think they have accepted
arrogance in the universe,
then bring them to gynecologists
not unlike themselves.

■

the mother's story

a line of women i don't know,
she said,
came in and whispered over you
each one fierce word,
she said, each word
more powerful than one before.
and i thought what is this to bring
to one black girl from buffalo
until the last one came and smiled,
she said,
and filled your ear with light
and that, she said, has been the one,
the last one, that last one.

∎

in which i consider the fortunate deaf

the language palpable,
their palm prints folded around
the names of the things.
seasons like skin
snuggled against fingerbone
and their wonder at loving
someone like you perhaps,
even your absence tangible,
your cold name fastened
into their shivering hands.

■

4/25/89   late

(f. diagnosed w. cancer 4/25/84)

when i awake
the time will have jerked back
into five years ago,
the sea will not be this one,
you will run
under a grayer sky
wearing that green knit cap
we laughed about
and, sweating home again
after your run, all fit
and well and safe, you will
prepare to meet that
stethoscopic group
and hear yourself pronounced
an almost ghost.

■

as he was dying
a canticle of birds
hovered
watching through the glass
as if to catch
that final breath
and sing it   where?
he died.
there was a shattering of wing
that sounded   then did not sound,
and we stood in this silence
blackly   some would say,
while through the windows,
as perhaps at other times,
the birds, if they had stayed,
could see us,
and i do not mean white here,
but as we are,
transparent women and transparent men.

■

night sound

the sound of a woman breathing
who has inhaled already
past her mother, who has left
behind more days than are ahead,
who must measure her exhalations
carefully, who spends these cries,
these soft expensive murmurings on you

man   breathing as if there could be
a surplus of air, of evening,
as if there could be even now
no question of tomorrow.

■

the spirit walks in
through the door
of the flesh's house

the rooms leading off
from the hall
burn with color

the spirit feels
the door behind her close

and the sinister hall
is thick with the one word
Choose

the poet walks
in through the door
of the scholar's house

the rooms leading off
from the hall
buzz with language

the poet
feels the door
behind her close

and the sinister hall
is dark with the one word
Choose

■

after the reading

tired from being a poet
i throw myself onto
Howard Johnson's bed
and long for home,
that sad mysterious country
where nobody notices
a word i say, nobody
thinks more of me or less
than they would think of any
chattering thing; mice
running toward the dark, leaves
rubbing against one another,
words tumbling together
up the long stair, home,
my own cheap lamp i can switch off
pretending i'm at peace there
in the dark. home. i sink at last into
the poet's short and fitful sleep.

■

moonchild

only after the death
of the man who killed the bear,
after the death of the coalminer's son,
did i remember that the moon
also rises, coming heavy or thin
over the living fields, over
the cities of the dead;
only then did i remember how she
catches the sun and keeps most of him
for the evening that surely will come;
and it comes.
only then did i know that to live
in the world all that i needed was
some small light and know that indeed
i would rise again and rise again to dance.

■

tree of life

How art thou fallen from Heaven,
O Lucifer, son of the morning? . . .
—Isaiah 14:12

oh where have you fallen to
son of the morning
beautiful lucifer
bringer of light
it is all shadow
in heaven without you
the cherubim sing
kaddish

and even the
solitary brother
has risen from his seat
of stones   he is holding
they say   a wooden stick
and pointing toward
a garden

light breaks
where no light was before
where no eye is prepared
to see
and animals rise up to walk
oh lucifer
what have you done

■

remembering the birth of lucifer

some will remember
the flash of light
as he broke
from the littlest finger
of God   some will
recall the bright shimmer
and then
flush in the tremble of air
so much shine

even then   the seraphim say
they knew
it was too much for
one small heaven
they rustled their three wings
they say   and began
to wait   and to watch

■

whispered to lucifer

lucifer six-finger
where have you gone to
with your swift lightning

oh son of the morning
was it the woman
enticed you to leave us

was it to touch her
featherless arm
was it to curl your belly

around her
that you fell laughing
your grace all ashard

leaving us here in
perpetual evening
even the guardians

silent   all of us
going about our
father's business

less radiant
less sure

■

eve's version

smooth talker
slides into my dreams
and fills them with apple
apple snug as my breast
in the palm of my hand
apple sleek apple sweet
and bright in my mouth

it is your own lush self
you hunger for
he whispers   lucifer
honey-tongue.

■

lucifer understanding at last

thy servant lord

bearer of lightning
and of lust

thrust between the
legs of the earth
into this garden

phallus and father
doing holy work

oh sweet delight
oh eden

if the angels
hear of this

there will be no peace
in heaven

■

the garden of delight

for some
it is stone
bare smooth
as a buttock
rounding
into the crevasse
of the world

for some
it is extravagant
water   mouths wide
washing together
forever   for some
it is fire
for some air

and for some
certain only of the syllables
it is the element they
search their lives for

eden

for them
it is a test

■

adam thinking

she
stolen from my bone
is it any wonder
i hunger to tunnel back
inside   desperate
to reconnect the rib and clay
and to be whole again

some need is in me
struggling to roar through my
mouth into a name
this creation is so fierce
i would rather have been born

■

eve thinking

it is wild country here
brothers and sisters coupling
claw and wing
groping one another

i wait
while the clay two-foot
rumbles in his chest
searching for language to

call me
but he is slow
tonight as he sleeps
i will whisper into his mouth
our names

■

the story thus far

so they went out
clay and morning star
following the bright back
of the woman

as she walked past
the cherubim
turning their fiery swords
past the winged gate

into the unborn world
chaos fell away
before her like a cloud
and everywhere seemed light

seemed glorious
seemed very eden

■

lucifer speaks in his own voice

sure as i am
of the seraphim
folding wing
so am i certain of a
graceful bed
and a soft caress
along my long belly
at endtime   it was
to be
i who was called son
if only of the morning
saw that some must
walk or all will crawl
so slithered into earth
and seized the serpent in
the animals   i became
the lord of snake for
adam and for eve
i   the only lucifer
light-bringer
created out of fire
illuminate i could
and so
illuminate i did

■

prayer

blessing the boats

(at St. Mary's)

may the tide
that is entering even now
the lip of our understanding
carry you out
beyond the face of fear
may you kiss
the wind then turn from it
certain that it will
love your back   may you
open your eyes to water
water waving forever
and may you in your innocence
sail through this to that

■

The Book of Light

(1992)

for kathy
your sister david

LIGHT

ray
stream
gleam
beam
sun
glow
flicker
shine
lucid
spark
scintilla
flash
blaze
flame
fire
serene
luciferous
lightning bolt
luster
shimmer
glisten
gloss
brightness
brilliance
splendor
sheen
dazzle
sparkle
luminous
reflection
kindle
illuminate
brighten
glorious

radiate
radiant
splendid
clarify
clear

ROGET'S THESAURUS

∎

reflection

climbing

a woman precedes me up the long rope,
her dangling braids the color of rain.
maybe i should have had braids.
maybe i should have kept the body i started,
slim and possible as a boy's bone.
maybe i should have wanted less.
maybe i should have ignored the bowl in me
burning to be filled.
maybe i should have wanted less.
the woman passes the notch in the rope
marked Sixty.   i rise toward it, struggling,
hand over hungry hand.

■

june 20

i will be born in one week
to a frowned forehead of a woman
and a man whose fingers will itch
to enter me. she will crochet
a dress for me of silver
and he will carry me in it.
they will do for each other
all that they can
but it will not be enough.
none of us know that we will not
smile again for years,
that she will not live long.
in one week i will emerge face first
into their temporary joy.

■

daughters

woman who shines at the head
of my grandmother's bed,
brilliant woman, i like to think
you whispered into her ear
instructions. i like to think
you are the oddness in us,
you are the arrow
that pierced our plain skin
and made us fancy women;
my wild witch gran, my magic mama,
and even these gaudy girls.
i like to think you gave us
extraordinary power and to
protect us, you became the name
we were cautioned to forget.
it is enough,
you must have murmured,
to remember that i was
and that you are. woman, i am
lucille, which stands for light,
daughter of thelma, daughter
of georgia, daughter of
dazzling you.

■

sam

if he could have kept
the sky in his dark hand
he would have pulled it down
and held it.
it would have called him lord
as did the skinny women
in virginia. if he
could have gone to school
he would have learned to write
his story and not live it.
if he could have done better
he would have. oh stars
and stripes forever,
what did you do to my father?

■

my lost father

see where he moves
he leaves a wake of tears
see in the path of his going
the banners of regret
see just above him the cloud
of welcome   see him rise
see him enter the company
of husbands   fathers   sons

■

thel

was my first landscape,
red brown as the clay
of her georgia.
sweet attic of a woman,
repository of old songs.
there was such music in her;
she would sit, shy as a wren
humming alone and lonely
amid broken promises,
amid the sweet broken bodies
of birds.

■

imagining bear

for alonzo moore sr.

imagine him too tall and too wide
for the entrance into parlors

imagine his hide gruff, the hair on him
grizzled even to his own hand

imagine his odor surrounding him,
rank and bittersweet as bark

imagine him lumbering as he moves
imagine his growl filling the wind

give him an old guitar
give him a bottle of booze

imagine his children laughing; papa   papa
imagine his wife sighing; oh lonnie

imagine him singing, imagine his granddaughter
remembering him in poems

■

c.c. rider

who is that running away
with my life? who is that
black horse, who is that rider
dressed like my sons, braided
like my daughters? who is that
georgia woman, who is that
virginia man, who is that light-eyed
stranger not looking back?
who is that hollow woman? who am i?
see see rider, see what you have done.

■

11/10 again

some say the radiance around the body
can be seen by eyes latticed against
all light but the particular. they say
you can notice something rise
from the houseboat of the body
wearing the body's face,
and that you can feel the presence
of a possible otherwhere.
not mystical, they say, but human,
human to lift away from the arms that
try to hold you (as you did then)
and, brilliance magnified,
circle beyond the ironwork
encasing your human heart.

■

she lived

after he died
what really happened is
she watched the days
bundle into thousands,
watched every act become
the history of others,
every bed more
narrow,
but even as the eyes of lovers
strained toward the milky young
she walked away
from the hole in the ground
deciding to live.   and she lived.

■

for roddy

i am imagining this of you,
turned away from breath
as you turned from my body,
refusing to defile what you adored;
i am imagining rejuvenated bones
rising from the dead floor where
they found you, rising and running
back into the life you loved,
dancing as you would dance
toward me, wherever, whose ever i am.

■

them and us

something in their psyche insists on elvis
slouching into markets, his great collar
high around his great head, his sideburns
extravagant, elvis, still swiveling those
negro hips. something needs to know

that even death, the most faithful manager
can be persuaded to give way
before real talent, that it is possible
to triumph forever on a timeless stage
surrounded by lovers giving the kid a hand.

we have so many gone. history
has taught us much about fame and its
inevitable tomorrow. we ride the subways
home from the picture show, sure about
death and elvis, but watching for marvin gaye.

■

the women you are accustomed to

wearing that same black dress,
their lips and asses tight;
their bronzed hair set in perfect place,
these women gathered in my dream
to talk their usual talk,
their conversation spiked with the names
of avenues in France.

and when i asked them what the hell,
they shook their marble heads
and walked erect out of my sleep,
back into a town which knows
all there is to know
about the cold outside, where i relaxed
and thought of you,
your burning blood, your dancing tongue.

■

song at midnight

> . . . do not
> send me out
> among strangers
>   —Sonia Sanchez

brothers,
this big woman
carries much sweetness
in the folds of her flesh.
her hair
is white with wonderful.
she is
rounder than the moon
and far more faithful.
brothers,
who will not hold her,
who will find her beautiful
if you do not?

■

won't you celebrate with me
what i have shaped into
a kind of life? i had no model.
born in babylon
both nonwhite and woman
what did i see to be except myself?
i made it up
here on this bridge between
starshine and clay,
my one hand holding tight
my other hand; come celebrate
with me that everyday
something has tried to kill me
and has failed.

■

lightning bolt

it was a dream

in which my greater self
rose up before me
accusing me of my life
with her extra finger
whirling in a gyre of rage
at what my days had come to.
what,
i pleaded with her, could i do,
oh what could i have done?
and she twisted her wild hair
and sparked her wild eyes
and screamed as long as
i could hear her
This.   This.   This.

■

each morning i pull myself
out of despair

from a night of coals and a tongue
blistered with smiling

the step past the mother bed
is a high step

the walk through the widow's door
is a long walk

and who are these voices calling
from every mirrored thing

say it coward say it

■

here yet be dragons

so many languages have fallen
off of the edge of the world
into the dragon's mouth. some

where there be monsters whose teeth
are sharp and sparkle with lost

people. lost poems. who
among us can imagine ourselves
unimagined? who

among us can speak with so fragile
tongue and remain proud?

■

the yeti poet returns to his village
to tell his story

. . . found myself wondering
if i had entered
the valley of shadow

found myself wandering
a shrunken world
of hairless men

oh the pouches
they close themselves into
at night   oh the thin
paps of their women

i turned from the click
of their spirit-catching box
the boom of their long stick

and made my way back
to this wilderness
where we know where we are
what we are

■

crabbing

(the poet crab speaks)

pulling
into their pots
our wives
our hapless children.
crabbing
they smile, meaning us
i imagine,
though our name
is our best secret.
this forward moving
fingered thing
inedible
even to itself,
how can it understand
the sweet sacred meat
of others?

■

the earth is a living thing

is a black shambling bear
ruffling its wild back and tossing
mountains into the sea

is a black hawk circling
the burying ground circling the bones
picked clean and discarded

is a fish black blind in the belly of water
is a diamond blind in the black belly of coal

is a black and living thing
is a favorite child
of the universe
feel her rolling her hand
in its kinky hair
feel her brushing it clean

■

move

*On May 13, 1985 Wilson Goode, Philadelphia's first Black
mayor, authorized the bombing of 6221 Osage Avenue
after the complaints of neighbors, also Black, about the
Afrocentric back-to-nature group headquartered there
and calling itself Move. All the members of the group
wore dreadlocks and had taken the surname Africa. In the
bombing eleven people, including children, were killed
and sixty-one homes in the neighborhood were destroyed.*

they had begun to whisper
among themselves   hesitant
to be branded neighbor to the wild
haired women the naked children
reclaiming a continent
away

move

he hesitated
then turned his smoky finger
toward africa toward the house
he might have lived in might have
owned or saved had he not turned
away

move

the helicopter rose at the command
higher at first then hesitating
then turning toward the center
of its own town only a neighborhood
away

move

she cried as the child stood
hesitant in the last clear sky
he would ever see   the last
before the whirling blades the whirling smoke
and sharp debris carried all clarity
away

move

if you live in a mind
that would destroy itself
to comfort itself
if you would stand fire
rather than difference
do not hesitate
move
away

■

samson predicts from gaza
the philadelphia fire

for ramona africa, survivor

it will be your hair
ramona africa
they will come for you
they will bring fire
they will empty your eyes
of everything you love
your hair will writhe
and hiss on your shoulder
they will order you
to give it up   if you do
you will bring the temple down
if you do not   they will

■

january 1991

they have sent our boy
to muffle himself
in the sand. our son
who has worshipped skin,
pale and visible as heaven,
all his life,
who has practiced the actual
name of God,
who knows himself to be
the very photograph of Adam.
yes, our best boy is there
with his bright-eyed sister,
both of them waiting in dunes
distant as Mars
to shutter the dark veiled lids
of not our kind.
they, who are not us, they have
no life we recognize,
no heaven we can care about,
no word for God we can pronounce.
we do not know them,
do not want to know them,
do not want this lying at night
all over the bare stone county
dreaming of desert for the first time
and of death and our boy and his sister
and them and us.

■

dear jesse helms,

something is happening.
something obscene.

in the night sky
the stars are bursting

into flame. thousands
and thousands of lights

are pouring down onto
the children of allah,

and jesse,

the smart bombs do not recognize
the babies. something

is happening obscene.

they are shrouding words so that
families cannot find them.

civilian deaths have become
collateral damage, bullets

are anti-personnel. jesse,
the fear is anti-personnel.

jesse, the hate is anti-personnel.
jesse, the war is anti-personnel,

and something awful is happening.
something obscene.

■

if i should

to clark kent

enter the darkest room
in my house and speak
with my own voice, at last,
about its awful furniture,
pulling apart the covering
over the dusty bodies; the randy
father, the husband holding ice
in his hand like a blessing,
the mother bleeding into herself
and the small imploding girl,
i say if i should walk into
that web, who will come flying
after me, leaping tall buildings?
you?

■

further note to clark

do you know how hard this is for me?
do you know what you're asking?

what i can promise to be is water,
water plain and direct as Niagara.
unsparing of myself, unsparing of
the cliff i batter, but also unsparing
of you, tourist. the question for me is
how long can i cling to this edge?
the question for you is
what have you ever traveled toward
more than your own safety?

■

begin here

in the dark
where the girl is
sleeping
begin with a shadow
rising on the wall
no
begin with a spear
of salt like a tongue
no
begin with a swollen
horn   or finger
no
no   begin here
something in the girl
is wakening   some
thing in the girl
is falling
deeper and deeper
asleep

■

night vision

the girl fits her body in
to the space between the bed
and the wall. she is a stalk,
exhausted. she will do some
thing with this. she will
surround these bones with flesh.
she will cultivate night vision.
she will train her tongue
to lie still in her mouth and listen.
the girl slips into sleep.
her dream is red and raging.
she will remember
to build something human with it.

■

fury

for mama

remember this.
she is standing by
the furnace.
the coals
glisten like rubies.
her hand is crying.
her hand is clutching
a sheaf of papers.
poems.
she gives them up.
they burn
jewels into jewels.
her eyes are animals.
each hank of her hair
is a serpent's obedient
wife.
she will never recover.
remember. there is nothing
you will not bear
for this woman's sake.

■

cigarettes

my father burned us all. ash
fell from his hand onto our beds,
onto our tables and chairs.
ours was the roof the sirens
rushed to at night
mistaking the glow of his pain
for flame. nothing is burning here,
my father would laugh, ignoring
my charred pillow, ignoring his own
smoldering halls.

■

final note to clark

they had it wrong,
the old comics.
you are only clark kent
after all. oh,
mild mannered mister,
why did i think you could fix it?
how you must have wondered
to see me taking chances,
dancing on the edge of words,
pointing out the bad guys,
dreaming your x-ray vision
could see the beauty in me.
what did i expect? what
did i hope for? we are who we are,
two faithful readers,
not wonder woman and not superman.

■

note, passed to superman

sweet jesus, superman,
if i had seen you
dressed in your blue suit
i would have known you.
maybe that choirboy clark
can stand around
listening to stories
but not you, not with
metropolis to save
and every crook in town
filthy with kryptonite.
lord, man of steel,
i understand the cape,
the leggings, the whole
ball of wax.
you can trust me,
there is no planet stranger
than the one i'm from.

■

love the human
                    —*Gary Snyder*

the rough weight of it
scarring its own back
the dirt under the fingernails
the bloody cock   love
the thin line secting the belly
the small gatherings
gathered in sorrow or joy
love the silences
love the terrible noise
love the stink of it
love it all   love
even the improbable foot   even
the surprised and ungrateful eye

■

splendor

seeker of visions

what does this mean
to see walking men
wrapped in the color of death,
to hear from their tongue
such difficult syllables?
are they the spirits
of our hope
or the pale ghosts of our future?
who will believe the red road
will not run on forever?
who will believe
a tribe of ice might live
and we might not?

columbus day '91

∎

Nothing is told us about Sisyphus in the underworld.
                                        —Albert Camus

nothing about the moment
just after the ball fits itself
into the bottom of the hill
and the world is suspended
and i become king of this country
all imps and imposters watching
me,
waiting me, and i decide, i decide
whether or not i will allow
this myth to live. i slide
myself down. demons restoke the
fire.
i push my shoulder into the round
world and taste in my mouth
how sweet power is, the story
gods never tell.

∎

atlas

i am used to the heft of it
sitting against my rib,
used to the ridges of forest,
used to the way my thumb
slips into the sea as i pull
it tight. something is sweet
in the thick odor of flesh
burning and sweating and bearing young.
i have learned to carry it
the way a poor man learns
to carry everything.

■

sarah's promise

who understands better than i
the hunger in old bones
for a son? so here we are,
abraham with his faith
and i my fury. jehovah,
i march into the thicket
of your need and promise you
the children of young women,
yours for a thousand years.
their faith will send them to you,
docile as abraham. now,
speak to my husband.
spare me my one good boy.

■

naomi watches as ruth sleeps

she clings to me
like a shadow
when all that i wish
is to sit alone
longing for my husband,
my sons.
she has promised
to follow me,
to become me
if i allow it.
i am leading her
to boaz country.
he will find her beautiful
and place her among
his concubines.
jehovah willing
i can grieve in peace.

■

cain

so this is what it means
to be an old man;
every member of my body
limp and unsatisfied,
father to sons who never knew
my father, husband to the
sister of the east,
and all night, in the rocky
land of nod,
listening to the thunderous
roll of voices,
unable to tell them where
my brother is.

■

leda   1

there is nothing luminous
about this.
they took my children.
i live alone in the backside
of the village.
my mother moved
to another town. my father
follows me around the well,
his thick lips slavering,
and at night my dreams are full
of the cursing of me
fucking god fucking me.

■

leda 2

a note on visitations

sometimes another star chooses.
the ones coming in from the east
are dagger-fingered men,
princes of no known kingdom.
the animals are raised up in their stalls
battering the stable door.
sometimes it all goes badly;
the inn is strewn with feathers,
the old husband suspicious,
and the fur between her thighs
is the only shining thing.

■

leda 3

a personal note (re: visitations)

always pyrotechnics;
stars spinning into phalluses
of light, serpents promising
sweetness, their forked tongues
thick and erect, patriarchs of bird
exposing themselves in the air.
this skin is sick with loneliness.
You want what a man wants,
next time come as a man
or don't come.

■

far memory

a poem in seven parts

1
convent

my knees recall the pockets
worn into the stone floor,
my hands, tracing against the wall
their original name, remember
the cold brush of brick, and the smell
of the brick powdery and wet
and the light finding its way in
through the high bars.

and also the sisters singing
at matins, their sweet music
the voice of the universe at peace
and the candles their light the light
at the beginning of creation
and the wonderful simplicity of prayer
smooth along the wooden beads
and certainly attended.

2
someone inside me remembers

that my knees must be hidden away
that my hair must be shorn
so that vanity will not test me
that my fingers are places of prayer
and are holy   that my body is promised
to something more certain
than myself

3
again

born in the year of war
on the day of perpetual help.

come from the house
of stillness
through the soft gate
of a silent mother.

come to a betraying father.
come to a husband who would one day
rise and enter a holy house.

come to wrestle with you again,
passion, old disobedient friend,
through the secular days and nights
of another life.

4
trying to understand this life

who did i fail, who
did i cease to protect
that i should wake each morning
facing the cold north?

perhaps there is a cart
somewhere in history
of children crying "sister
save us" as she walks away.

the woman walks into my dreams
dragging her old habit.
i turn from her, shivering,

to begin another afternoon
of rescue, rescue.

5
sinnerman

horizontal one evening
on the cold stone,
my cross burning into
my breast, did i dream
through my veil
of his fingers digging
and is this the dream
again, him, collarless
over me, calling me back
to the stones of this world
and my own whispered
hosanna?

6
karma

the habit is heavy.
you feel its weight
pulling around your ankles
for a hundred years.

the broken vows
hang against your breasts,
each bead a word
that beats you.

even now
to hear the words
defend

protect
goodbye
lost or
alone
is to be washed in sorrow.

and in this life
there is no retreat
no sanctuary
no whole abiding
sister.

7
gloria mundi

so knowing,
what is known?
that we carry our baggage
in our cupped hands
when we burst through
the waters of our mother.
that some are born
and some are brought
to the glory of this world.
that it is more difficult
than faith
to serve only one calling
one commitment
one devotion
in one life.

■

brothers

*(being a conversation in eight poems between an aged
Lucifer and God, though only Lucifer is heard. The time is
long after.)*

1
invitation

come coil with me
here in creation's bed
among the twigs and ribbons
of the past. i have grown old
remembering this garden,
the hum of the great cats
moving into language, the sweet
fume of man's rib
as it rose up and began to walk.
it was all glory then,
the winged creatures leaping
like angels, the oceans claiming
their own. let us rest here a time
like two old brothers
who watched it happen and wondered
what it meant.

2
how great Thou art

listen, You are beyond
even Your own understanding.
that rib and rain and clay
in all its pride,
its unsteady dominion,

is not what You believed
You were,
but it is what You are;
in Your own image as some
lexicographer supposed.
the face, both he and she,
the odd ambition, the desire
to reach beyond the stars
is You. all You, all You
the loneliness, the perfect
imperfection.

3
as for myself

less snake than angel
less angel than man
how come i to this
serpent's understanding?
watching creation from
a hood of leaves
i have foreseen the evening
of the world.
as sure as she,
the breast of Yourself
separated out and made to bear,
as sure as her returning,
i too am blessed with
the one gift you cherish;
to feel the living move in me
and to be unafraid.

4

in my own defense

what could i choose
but to slide along beside them,
they whose only sin
was being their father's children?
as they stood with their backs
to the garden,
a new and terrible luster
burning their eyes,
only You could have called
their ineffable names,
only in their fever
could they have failed to hear.

5

the road led from delight

into delight. into the sharp
edge of seasons, into the sweet
puff of bread baking, the warm
vale of sheet and sweat after love,
the tinny newborn cry of calf
and cormorant and humankind.
and pain, of course,
always there was some bleeding,
but forbid me not
my meditation on the outer world
before the rest of it, before
the bruising of his heel, my head,
and so forth.

6

"the silence of God is God."

—Carolyn Forché

tell me, tell us why
in the confusion of a mountain
of babies stacked like cordwood,
of limbs walking away from each other,
of tongues bitten through
by the language of assault,
tell me, tell us why
You neither raised Your hand
nor turned away, tell us why
You watched the excommunication of
that world and You said nothing.

7

still there is mercy, there is grace

how otherwise
could i have come to this
marble spinning in space
propelled by the great
thumb of the universe?
how otherwise
could the two roads
of this tongue
converge into a single
certitude?
how otherwise
could i, a sleek old
traveler,
curl one day safe and still
beside You
at Your feet, perhaps,
but, amen, Yours.

8
"............is God."

so.
having no need to speak
You sent Your tongue
splintered into angels.
even i,
with my little piece of it
have said too much.
to ask You to explain
is to deny You.
before the word
You were.
You kiss my brother mouth.
the rest is silence.

∎

Uncollected Poems

(1993)

hometown
1993

think of it; the landscape
potted as if by war, think of
the weeds, the boarded buildings,
the slivers of window abandoned
in the streets, and behind one
glass, my little brother, dying.
think of how he must have
bounded into our mothers arms,
held hard to our fathers swollen hand,
never looking back, glad to be gone
from the contempt, the terrible night
of buffalo.

■

ones like us

enter a blurry world,
fetish tight around our
smallest finger, mezuzah
gripped in our good child hand.
we feel for our luck
but everywhere is menace   menace
until we settle ourselves
against the bark of trees, against
the hide of fierce protection
and there, in the shadow,
words call us.   words call us
and we go.

for wayne karlin
5/28/93

■

The Terrible Stories

(1996)

for marilyn marlow

telling our stories

the fox came every evening to my door
asking for nothing. my fear
trapped me inside, hoping to dismiss her
but she sat till morning, waiting.

at dawn we would, each of us,
rise from our haunches, look through the glass
then walk away.

did she gather her village around her
and sing of the hairless moon face,
the trembling snout, the ignorant eyes?

child, i tell you now it was not
the animal blood i was hiding from,
it was the poet in her, the poet and
the terrible stories she could tell.

■

1. A Dream of Foxes

fox

. . . The foxes are hungry, who could blame them
for what they do? . . .
— *"Foxesin Winter"*
Mary Oliver

who
can blame her for hunkering
into the doorwells at night,
the only blaze in the dark
the brush of her hopeful tail,
the only starlight
her little bared teeth?

and when she is not satisfied
who can blame her for refusing to leave,
for raising the one paw up and barking,
Master Of The Hunt, why am i
not feeding, not being fed?

■

the coming of fox

one evening i return
to a red fox
haunched by my door.

i am afraid
although she knows
no enemy comes here.

next night again
then next then next
she sits in her safe shadow

silent as my skin bleeds
into long bright flags
of fur.

■

dear fox

it is not my habit
to squat in the hungry desert
fingering stones, begging them
to heal, not me but the dry mornings
and bitter nights.
it is not your habit
to watch. none of this
is ours, sister fox.
tell yourself that anytime now
we will rise and walk away
from somebody else's life.
any time.

■

leaving fox

so many fuckless days and nights.
only the solitary fox
watching my window light
barks her compassion.
i move away from her eyes,
from the pitying brush
of her tail
to a new place and check
for signs. so far
i am the only animal.
i will keep the door unlocked
until something human comes.

■

one year later

what if,
then,
entering my room,
brushing against the shadows,
lapping them into rust,
her soft paw extended,
she had called me out?
what if,
then,
i had reared up baying,
and followed her off
into vixen country?
what then of the moon,
the room, the bed, the poetry
of regret?

■

a dream of foxes

in the dream of foxes
there is a field
and a procession of women
clean as good children
no hollow in the world
surrounded by dogs
no fur clumped bloody
on the ground
only a lovely line
of honest women stepping
without fear or guilt or shame
safe through the generous fields

■

2. From the Cadaver

amazons

when the rookery of women
warriors all
each cupping one hand around
her remaining breast

daughters of dahomey
their name fierce on the planet

when they came to ask
who knows what you might have
to sacrifice   poet   amazon
there is no choice

then when they each
with one nipple lifted
beckoned to me
five generations removed

i rose
and ran to the telephone
to hear
    cancer   early detection   no
    mastectomy   not yet

there was nothing to say
my sisters swooped in a circle dance
audre was with them and i
had already written this poem

■

lumpectomy eve

all night i dream of lips
that nursed and nursed
and the lonely nipple

lost in loss and the need
to feed that turns at last
on itself   that will kill

its body for its hunger's sake
all night i hear the whispering
the soft

     love calls you to this knife
     for love   for love

all night it is the one breast
comforting the other

■

consulting the book of changes:
radiation

each morning you will cup
your breast in your hand
then cover it and ride
into the federal city.

    if there are no cherry blossoms
    can there be a cherry tree?

you will arrive at the house
of lightning. even the children there
will glow in the arms of their kin.

    where is the light in one leaf
    falling?

you will wait to hear your name,
wish you were a child with kin,
wish some of the men you loved
had loved you.

    what is the splendor of one breast
    on one woman?

you will rise to the machine.
if someone should touch you now
his hand would flower.

after, you will stop to feed yourself.
you have always had to feed yourself.

will i begin to cry?

if you do, you will cry forever.

■

1994

i was leaving my fifty-eighth year
when a thumb of ice
stamped itself hard near my heart

you have your own story
you know about the fear the tears
the scar of disbelief

you know that the saddest lies
are the ones we tell ourselves
you know how dangerous it is

to be born with breasts
you know how dangerous it is
to wear dark skin

i was leaving my fifty-eighth year
when i woke into the winter
of a cold and mortal body

thin icicles hanging off
the one mad nipple weeping

have we not been good children
did we not inherit the earth

but you must know all about this
from your own shivering life

■

scar

we will learn
to live together.

i will call you
ribbon of hunger
and desire
empty pocket flap
edge of before and after.

and you
what will you call me?

woman i ride
who cannot throw me
and i will not fall off.

■

hag riding

why
is what i ask myself
maybe it is the afrikan in me
still trying to get home
after all these years
but when i wake to the heat of the morning
galloping down the highway of my life
something hopeful rises in me
rises and runs me out into the road
and i lob my fierce thigh high
over the rump of the day and honey
i ride   i ride

■

down the tram

hell is like this   first stone
then rock so wonderful
you forget you have no faith
some pine   some scrub brush
just enough to clench green
in the air
yes   it is always evening
there are stars   there is sky
you stand there silent
in the long approach
watching as caverns
tense into buildings
wondering who could live here
knowing whatever they have done
they must be beautiful

■

rust

we don't like rust,
it reminds us that we are dying.
—Brett Singer

are you saying that iron understands
time is another name for God?

that the rain-licked pot is holy?
that the pan abandoned in the house

is holy? are you saying that they
are sanctified now, our girlhood skillets

tarnishing in the kitchen?
are you saying we only want to remember

the heft of our mothers' handles,
their ebony patience, their shine?

■

from the cadaver

for bill palmer

the arm you hold up
held a son   he became
taller than his father
if he is watching there
in my dim lit past
let him see
what a man comes to
doctor or patient
criminal or king
pieces of baggage
cold in a stranger's hand

■

3. A Term in Memphis

shadows

in the latter days
you will come to a place
called memphis
there you will wait for a while
by the river mississippi
until you can feel the shadow
of another memphis and another
river. nile

wake up girl.
you dreaming.

the sign may be water or fire
or it may be the black earth
or the black blood under the earth
or it may be the syllables themselves
coded to you from your southern kin.

wake up girl.
i swear you dreaming.

memphis.
capital of the old kingdom
of ancient egypt at the apex
of the river across from
the great pyramids.
nile. born in the mountains
of the moon.

wake up girl,
this don't connect.

wait there.
in the shadow of your room

you may see another dusky woman
weakened by too much loss.
she will be dreaming a small boat
through centuries of water
into the white new world.
she will be weaving garments
of neglect.

wake up girl.
this don't mean nothing.

meaning is the river
of voices. meaning
is the patience of the moon.
meaning is the thread
running forever in shadow.

girl girl wake up.
somebody calling you.

■

slaveships

loaded like spoons
into the belly of Jesus
where we lay for weeks for months
in the sweat and stink
of our own breathing
Jesus
why do you not protect us
chained to the heart of the Angel
where the prayers we never tell
and hot and red
as our bloody ankles
Jesus
Angel
can these be men
who vomit us out from ships
called Jesus   Angel   Grace Of God
onto a heathen country
Jesus
Angel
ever again
can this tongue speak
can these bones walk
Grace Of God
can this sin live

■

entering the south

i have put on my mother's coat.
it is warm and familiar
as old fur
and i can hear hushed voices
through it.   too many
animals have died
to make this.   the sleeves
coil down toward my hands
like rope.   i will wear it
because she loved it
but the blood from it pools
on my shoulders
heavy and dark and alive.

■

the mississippi river empties into the gulf

and the gulf enters the sea and so forth,
none of them emptying anything,
all of them carrying yesterday
forever on their white tipped backs,
all of them dragging forward tomorrow.
it is the great circulation
of the earth's body, like the blood
of the gods, this river in which the past
is always flowing. every water
is the same water coming round.
everyday someone is standing on the edge
of this river, staring into time,
whispering mistakenly:
only here. only now.

■

old man river

everything elegant
but this water

tables set with crystal
at the tea shop

miss lady patting her lips
with linen

horses pure stock
negras pure stock

everything clear
but this big muddy

water

don't say nothin'
must know somethin'

■

Beckwith found guilty of shooting Medgar
Evers in the back, killing him in 1963.
—newspaper 2/94

the son of medgar
will soon be
older than medgar

he came he says
to show in this courtroom
medgar's face

the old man sits
turned toward his old wife
then turns away

he is sick
his old wife sighs
he is only a sick old man

medgar isn't
wasn't
won't be

■

auction street

for angela mcdonald

consider the drum.
consider auction street
and the beat
throbbing up through our shoes,
through the trolley
so that it rides as if propelled
by hundreds, by thousands
of fathers and mothers
led in a coffle
to the block.

consider the block,
topside smooth as skin
almost translucent like a drum
that has been beaten
for the last time
and waits now to be honored
for the music it has had to bear.
then consider brother moses,
who heard from the mountaintop:
take off your shoes,
the ground you walk is holy.

■

memphis

. . . at the river i stand,
guide my feet, hold my hand

i was raised
on the shore
of lake erie
e is for escape

.

there are more s'es
in mississippi
than my mother had
sons

this river never knew
the kingdom of dahomey

the first s
begins in slavery
and ends in y
on the bluffs

of memphis
why are you here
the river wonders
northern born

looking across from buffalo
you look into canada   toronto
is the name of the lights
burning at night

the bottom of memphis
drops into the nightmare
of a little girl's fear
in fifteen minutes

they could be here
i could be there
mississippi
not the river   the state

schwerner
and chaney
and goodman

medgar

schwerner
and chaney
and goodman
and medgar

my mother had one son
he died gently near lake erie

some rivers flow back
toward the beginning
i never learned to swim

will i float or drown
in this memphis
on the mississippi river

what is this southland
what has this to do with egypt
or dahomey
or with me

so many questions
northern born

■

what comes after this

water earth fire air
i can scarcely remember
gushing down through my mother
onto the family bed
but the dirt of eviction
is still there
and the burning bodies of men
i have tried to love

through the southern blinds
narrow memories enter the room
i had not counted on ice
nor clay nor the uncertain hiss
of an old flame   water earth fire
it is always unexpected and
i wonder what is coming
after this   whether it is air
or it is nothing

■

blake

saw them glittering in the trees,
their quills erect among the leaves,
angels everywhere. we need new words
for what this is, this hunger entering our
loneliness like birds, stunning our eyes into rays
of hope. we need the flutter that can save
us, something that will swirl across the face
of what we have become and bring us grace.
back north, i sit again in my own home
dreaming of blake, searching the branches
for just one poem.

■

4. In the Meantime

evening and my dead once husband
rises up from the spirit board
through trembled air   i moan
the names of our wayward sons
and ask him to explain   why
i fuss like a fishwife   why
cancer and terrible loneliness
and the wars against our people
and the room glimmers as if washed
in tears and out of the mist a hand
becomes flesh and i watch
as its pointing fingers spell

it does not help to know

■

memory

ask me to tell how it feels
remembering your mother's face
turned to water under the white words
of the man at the shoe store. ask me,
though she tells it better than i do,
not because of her charm
but because it never happened
she says,
no bully salesman swaggering,
no rage, no shame, none of it
ever happened.
i only remember buying you
your first grown up shoes
she smiles. ask me
how it feels.

■

my sanctified grandmother
spoke in tongues
dancing the syllables
down the aisle.

she leaned on light
as she sashayed through
the church hall conversing
with angels.

only now, grown away
from embarrassment,
only now do i beseech her,

i, who would ask the seraphim
to speak to me in my own words:

grandmother
help them to enter
my mouth.   teach me
to lean on understanding.
not my own.   theirs.

■

lee

my mother's people
belonged to the lees
my father would say
then spout a litany
of names   old lighthorse harry
old robert e

my father
who lied on his deathbed
who knew the truth
but didn't always choose it
who saw himself an honorable man

was proud of lee
that man of honor
praised by grant and lincoln
worshipped by his men
revered by the state of virginia
which he loved almost as much
as my father did

it may have been a lie
it may have been
one of my father's tales
if so there was an honor in it
if he was indeed to be
the child of slaves
he would decide himself
that proud old man

i can see him now
chaining his mother to lee

■

album

12/2/92

this lucky old man
is my father.   he is
waving and walking away
from damage he has done.
he is dressed in his good
gray hat, his sunday suit.
he knows himself to be
a lucky man.

today
is his birthday somewhere.
he is ninety.
what he has forgotten
is more than i have seen.
what i have forgotten
is more than i can bear.
he is my father,
our father,
and all of us still love him.
i turn the page, marveling,
jesus christ
what a lucky old man!

■

what did she know, when did she know it

in the evenings
what it was the soft tap tap
into the room   the cold curve
of the sheet arced off
the fingers sliding in
and the hard clench against the wall
before and after
all the cold air   cold edges
why the little girl never smiled
they are supposed to know everything
our mothers   what did she know
when did she know it

■

in the same week

for samuel sayles, jr., 1938–1993

after the third day
the fingers of your folded hands
must have melted together
into perpetual prayer.
it was hot and buffalo.
nothing innocent could stay.

in the same week
stafford folded his tongue
and was gone. nothing
innocent is safe.

the frailty of love
falls from the newspaper
onto our bedroom floor
and we walk past not noticing.
the end of something simple
is happening here,

something essential. brother,
we burned you into little shells
and stars. we hold them hard,
attend too late to each,
mourn every necessary bit.
the angels shake their heads.
too little and too late.

■

heaven

my brother is crouched at the edge
looking down.
he has gathered a circle of cloudy
friends around him
and they are watching the world.

i can feel them there, i always could.
i used to try to explain to him
the afterlife,
and he would laugh. he is laughing now,

pointing toward me. "she was my sister,"
i feel him say,
"even when she was right, she was wrong."

■

lorena

it lay in my palm soft and trembled
as a new bird and i thought about
authority and how it always insisted
on itself, how it was master
of the man, how it measured him, never
was ignored or denied and how it promised
there would be sweetness if it was obeyed
just like the saints do, like the angels,
and i opened the window and held out my
uncupped hand. i swear to god,
i thought it could fly

■

in the meantime

Poem ending with a line from The Mahabharata,
quoted at the time of the first atomic blast.

the Lord of loaves and fishes
frowns as the children of
Haiti Somalia Bosnia Rwanda Everyhere
float onto the boats of their bellies
and die   in the meantime
someone who is not hungry sits to dine

we could have become
fishers of men
we could have been
a balm
a light
we have become
not what we were

in the mean time
that split apart with the atom
all roads began to lead
to these tables
these hungry children
this time
and

I am become Death   the destroyer of worlds.

■

5. From the Book of David

for anne caston

dancer

i have ruled
for forty years,
seven in hebron
thiry-three in jerusalem.

i have lain under the stars
and dreamed of foreign women.
i have dreamed my legs around them,
dancing.

some nights,
holding them in the dream,
i would feel us
swallowed by the sky.

lately i have begun to bed
with virgins,
their round breasts warm
to an old man.

i hold my seed
still plentiful as stars.
it is not my time.

somewhere something is choosing.
i can feel it dancing in me,
something to do with
virgins and with stars.

i am grown old and full of days.
my thighs are trembling.
what will the world remember,

what matters to time,
i wonder,
the dancer or the dance?

■

son of jesse

my father had eight sons
seven for keeping

somewhere there is a chronicle
naming my mother

how could i be womantrue
dancing in a house of men

even when i gathered
foreign wives and concubines

i would tend them as i tended
sheep

but when i ripped my robe
and wailed and wept upon the earth

i was grieving for men and i knew it
for my Lord my brothers fathers sons

■

david has slain his ten thousands

i would rise from my covering
and walk at night
to escape the ten thousand
bloody voices

yet i am a man
after God's own heart

when i hung the hands
of my enemy to the square
they came to clutch my dreams
at night

what does He love,
my wrath or my regret?

■

to michal

Michal . . . looked through a window and saw
King David leaping and dancing before the
Lord; and she despised him in her heart.
                                    —II Samuel 6:16

moving and moaning
under our coverings
i could only guess
what women know
but wife
in the open arms of God
i became man and woman
filling and emptying
all at once
and oh the astonishment
of seed
dancing on the ground
as i leaped and turned
surrendering
not what i had withheld from you
but michal from myself.

■

enemies

for wayne karlin

evening.
i creep
into the tent
of saul.

for his sake
i have learned
the taste of blood.
in battle
i would drink his
and he mine.

we have become
enemies

yet here
he is an old man
sleeping
or my father.

i will remove
his armaments
his sword
his shield.

come morning
he will know himself
naked but alive

and i will remember
myself also. david.
the poet david.

∎

beloved

jonathan the son of saul
did love me
and michal the daughter of saul
did love me
and israel and judah all
and honey was heaped upon my head
and the sword of goliath the giant
was given into my hand
and every harp and timbrel sang with
what doth thy soul desire
and i did not know

until one eventide i walked out
onto the roof of the king's house

■

bathsheba

how it was   it was
as if all of the blood in my body
gorged
into my loin
so that even my fingers grew stiff
but cold
and the heat of my rod
was my only burning
desire
desire my only fire
and whether i loved her
i could not say but
i wanted her whatever she was
whether a curse
or the wife of uriah

■

the prophet

came to me
with a poor man's tale
of his one ewe lamb
sworn to him by seven
pieces of gold

and a tale of the greed
of a rich man
hungry for not his own
supper
who stole that lamb

and i in my arrogance
did swear by the fate
of my house and my kingdom
vengeance

oh the crack in my heart
when the prophet tolled
david
thou art the man

■

oh absalom my son my son

even as i turned myself from you
i longed to hold you oh
my wild haired son

running in the wilderness away
from me from us
into a thicket you could not foresee

if you had stayed
i feared you would kill me
if you left i feared you would die

oh my son
my son
what does the Lord require

■

david, musing

it was i who faced the lion and the bear
who gathered the five smooth stones
and the name of the first was hunger
and the name of the second was faith
and the name of the third was lyric
and passion the fourth and the fifth
was the stone of my regret   it was hunger
that brought the gore of the giant's head
into my hand
the others i fastened under my tongue
for later   for her   for israel   for my sons

■

what manner of man

if i am not singing to myself
to whom then?   each sound, each word
is a way of wondering that first
brushed against me in the hills
when i was an unshorn shepherd boy.
each star that watched my watching then
was a mouth that would not speak.

what is a man? what am i?

even when i am dancing now i am dancing
myself onto the tongue of heaven
hoping to move into some sure
answer from the Lord.
how can this david love himself,
be loved (i am singing and spinning now)
if he stands in the tents of history
bloody skull in one hand, harp in the other?

■

Blessing the Boats

(2000)

for Russell
1963–1997

the beautiful boy
has entered
the beautiful city

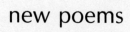

new poems

the times

it is hard to remain human on a day
when birds perch weeping
in the trees and the squirrel eyes
do not look away but the dog ones do
in pity.
another child has killed a child
and i catch myself relieved that they are
white and i might understand except
that i am tired of understanding.
if this
alphabet could speak its own tongue
it would be all symbol surely;
the cat would hunch across the long table
and that would mean time is catching up,
and the spindle fish would run to ground
and that would mean the end is coming
and the grains of dust would gather themselves
along the streets and spell out:

these too are your children   this too is your child

■

signs

■

when the birds begin to walk
when the crows in their silk tuxedos
stand in the road and watch
as oncoming traffic swerves to avoid
the valley of dead things
when the geese reject the sky
and sit on the apron of highway 95
one wing pointing north the other south

and what does it mean this morning
when a man runs wild eyed from his car
shirtless and shoeless his palms spread wide
into the jungle of traffic into a world
gone awry the birds beginning to walk
the man almost naked almost cawing
almost lifting straining to fly

■

moonchild

whatever slid into my mother's room that
late june night, tapping her great belly,
summoned me out roundheaded and unsmiling.
is this the moon, my father used to grin,
cradling me?   it was the moon
but nobody knew it then.

the moon understands dark places.
the moon has secrets of her own.
she holds what light she can.

we girls were ten years old and giggling
in our hand-me-downs. we wanted breasts,
pretended that we had them, tissued
our undershirts. jay johnson is teaching
me to french kiss, ella bragged, who
is teaching you? how do you say; my father?

the moon is queen of everything.
she rules the oceans, rivers, rain.
when I am asked whose tears these are
I always blame the moon.

■

dialysis

after the cancer, the kidneys
refused to continue.
they closed their thousand eyes.

blood fountains from the blind man's
arm and decorates the tile today.
somebody mops it up.

the woman who is over ninety
cries for her mother.   if our dead
were here they would save us.

we are not supposed to hate
the dialysis unit.   we are not
supposed to hate the universe.

this is not supposed to happen to me.
after the cancer the body refused
to lose any more.   even the poisons
were claimed and kept

until they threatened to destroy
the heart they loved.   in my dream
a house is burning.

something crawls out of the fire
cleansed and purified.
in my dream i call it light.

after the cancer i was so grateful
to be alive.   i am alive and furious.
Blessed be even this?

■

donor

to lex

when they tell me that my body
might reject
i think of thirty years ago
and the hangers i shoved inside
hard trying to not have you.

i think of the pills, the everything
i gathered against your
inconvenient bulge; and you
my stubborn baby child,
hunched there in the dark
refusing my refusal.

suppose my body does say no
to yours.   again, again i feel you
buckled in despite me, lex,
fastened to life like the frown
on an angel's brow.

■

libation

north carolina, 1999

i offer to this ground,
this gin.
i imagine an old man
crying here
out of the overseer's sight,

pushing his tongue
through where a tooth
would be if he were whole.
the space aches
where his tooth would be,

where his land would be, his
house   his wife   his son
his beautiful daughter.

he wipes his sorrow from
his cheek, then
puts his thirsty finger
to his thirsty tongue
and licks the salt.

i call a name that
could be his.
this offering
is for you old man;
this salty ground,
this gin.

■

the photograph: a lynching

is it the cut glass
of their eyes
looking up toward
the new gnarled branch
of the black man
hanging from a tree?

is it the white milk pleated
collar of the woman
smiling toward the camera,
her fingers loose around
a christian cross drooping
against her breast?

is it all of us
captured by history into an
accurate album? will we be
required to view it together
under a gathering sky?

■

jasper   texas   1998

for j. byrd

i am a man's head hunched in the road.
i was chosen to speak by the members
of my body.   the arm as it pulled away
pointed toward me, the hand opened once
and was gone.

why and why and why
should i call a white man brother?
who is the human in this place,
the thing that is dragged or the dragger?
what does my daughter say?

the sun is a blister overhead.
if i were alive i could not bear it.
the townsfolk sing we shall overcome
while hope bleeds slowly from my mouth
into the dirt that covers us all.
i am done with this dust.   i am done.

■

alabama 9/15/63

Have you heard the one about
the shivering lives,
the never to be borne daughters and sons,

the one about Cynthia and Carole and Denise and Addie
Mae?
Have you heard the one about
the four little birds
shattered into skylarks in the white
light of Birmingham?

Have you heard how the skylarks,
known for their music,
swooped into heaven, how the sunday
morning strains shook the piano, how the blast
is still too bright to hear them play?

■

what i think when i ride the train

maybe my father
made these couplers.
his hands were hard
and black and swollen,
the knuckles like lugs
or bolts in a rich man's box.
he broke a bone each year
as if on schedule.
when i read about a wreck,
how the cars buckle
together or hang from the track
in a chain, but never separate,
i think; see,
there's my father,
he was a chipper,
he made the best damn couplers
in the whole white world.

■

praise song

to my aunt blanche
who rolled from grass to driveway
into the street one sunday morning.
i was ten.   i had never seen
a human woman hurl her basketball
of a body into the traffic of the world.
Praise to the drivers who stopped in time.
Praise to the faith with which she rose
after some moments then slowly walked
sighing back to her family.
Praise to the arms which understood
little or nothing of what it meant
but welcomed her in without judgment,
accepting it all like children might,
like God.

■

august

for laine

what would we give,
my sister,
to roll our weak
and foolish brother

back onto his bed,
to face him with his sins
and blame him
for them?

what would we give
to fuss with him again,
he who clasped his hands
as if in prayer and melted

to our mother?   what
would we give
to smile and staple him
back into our arms,

our honey boy, our sam,
not clean, not sober, not
better than he was, but
oh, at least, alive?

■

study the masters

like my aunt timmie.
it was her iron,
or one like hers,
that smoothed the sheets
the master poet slept on.
home or hotel, what matters is
he lay himself down on her handiwork
and dreamed.   she dreamed too, words:
some cherokee, some masai and some
huge and particular as hope.
if you had heard her
chanting as she ironed
you would understand form and line
and discipline and order and
america.

■

lazarus

first day

i rose from stiffening
into a pin of light
and a voice calling
"Lazarus, this way"
and i floated or rather
swam in a river of sound
toward what seemed to be
forever   i was almost
almost there when i heard
behind me
"Lazarus, come forth" and
i found myself twisting
in the light for this
is the miracle, mary martha;
at my head and at my feet
singing my name
was the same voice

■

lazarus

second day

i am not the same man
borne into the crypt.

as ones return from otherwhere
altered by what they have seen,

so have i been forever.
lazarus.
lazarus who was dead.

what entered the light was one man.
what walked out is another.

■

lazarus

third day

on the third day i contemplate
what i was moving from
what i was moving toward

light again and
i could hear the seeds
turning in the grass   mary
martha i could feel the world

now i sit here in a crevice
on this rock   stared at
answering questions

sisters stand away
from the door to my grave
the only truth i know

■

birthday 1999

it is late.   the train
that is coming is
closer.   a woman can hear it
in her fingers, in her knees,
in the space where her uterus
was.   the platform feels
filled with people
but she sees no one else.
she can almost hear the
bright train eye.
she can almost touch the cracked
seat labeled lucille.
someone should be with her.
someone should undress her
stroke her one more time
and the train
keeps coming closer.

it is a dream i am having
more and more and more.

■

grief

begin with the pain
of the grass
that bore the weight
of adam,
his broken rib mending
into eve,

imagine
the original bleeding,
adam moaning
and the lamentation of grass.

from that garden,
through fields of lost
and found, to now, to here,
to grief for the upright
animal, to grief for the
horizontal world.

pause then for the human
animal in its coat
of many colors.   pause
for the myth of america.
pause for the myth
of america.

and pause for the girl
with twelve fingers
who never learned to cry enough
for anything that mattered,

not enough for the fear,
not enough for the loss,
not enough for the history,

not enough
for the disregarded planet.
not enough for the grass.

then end in the garden of regret
with time's bell tolling grief
and pain,
grief for the grass
that is older than adam,
grief for what is born human,
grief for what is not.

∎

report from the angel of eden

i found them there
rubbing against the leaves
so that the nubs of their
wings were flush under their skin

and it seemed like dancing
as when we angels
praise among the clouds
but they were not praising You

i watched
the grass grow soft and rich
under their luminous bodies
and their halos begin to fade

it was like dancing
creation flowered around them
moaning with delight   they were
trembling and i knew

a world was being born
i feared for their immortality
i feared for mine
under the strain of such desire

i knew
they could do evil
with it and i knew
they would

when i remembered what i was
i swiveled back unto Your grace
still winged i think but wondering
what now becomes   what now

of Paradise

Mercy

(2004)

Always Rica   1961–2000
Always Chan   1962–2004

". . . the only mercy is memory"

last words

the gift

there was a woman who hit her head
and ever after she could see the sharp
wing of things   blues and greens
radiating from the body of her sister
her mother   her friends   when she felt

in her eyes the yellow sting
of her mothers dying   she trembled
but did not speak   her bent brain
stilled her tongue so that her life
became flash after flash of silence

bright as flame   she is gone now
her head knocked again against a door
that opened for her only
i saw her last in a plain box smiling
behind her sewn eyes there were hints
of purple and crimson and gold

■

out of body

(mama)

the words
they fade
i sift
toward other languages
you must listen
with your hands
with the twist ends
of your hair
that leaf
pick up
the sharp green stem
try to feel me feel you
i am saying I still love you
i am saying
i am trying to say
i am trying to say
from my mouth
but baby there is no
mouth

■

dying

i saw a small moon rise
from the breast of a woman
lying in a hospital hall
and I saw that the moon was me
and I saw that the punctured bag
of a woman body was me
and i saw you sad there in the lobby
waiting to visit and I wanted
to sing to you
go home
i am waiting for you there

■

last words

(mama)

i am unforming
out of flesh

into the rubble
of the ground

there will be
new scars new tests

new "Mamas"
coming around

■

oh antic God
return to me
my mother in her thirties
leaned across the front porch
the huge pillow of her breasts
pressing against the rail
summoning me in for bed.

I am almost the dead woman's age times two.

I can barely recall her song
the scent of her hands
though her wild hair scratches my dreams
at night.   return to me, oh Lord of then
and now, my mother's calling,
her young voice humming my name.

■

april

bird and bird
over the thawing river
circling   parker
waving his horn
in the air above the osprey's
nest   my child
smiling her I know something
smile   their birthday
is coming   they are trying
to be forty   they will fail
they will fall
each from a different year
into the river   into the bay
into an ocean of marvelous things

∎

after one year

she who was beautiful
entered Lake-Too-Soon without warning us
that it would storm in
our hearts forever   that it would
alter the landscape of our lives
and that at night we would
fold ourselves into
towels into blankets anything
trying to stop our eyes
from drowning themselves

■

sonku

his heart, they said, was
three times the regular size.
yes, i said, i know.

■

children

they are right, the poet mother
carries her wolf in her heart,
wailing at pain yet suckling it like
romulus and remus.   this now.
how will I forgive myself
for trying to bear the weight of this
and trying to bear the weight also
of writing the poem
about this?

■

stories

surely i am able to write poems
celebrating grass and how the blue
in the sky can flow green or red
and the waters lean against the
chesapeake shore like a familiar,
poems about nature and landscape
surely   but whenever i begin
"the trees wave their knotted branches
and . . ."   why
is there under that poem always
an other poem?

■

mulberry fields

they thought the field was wasting
and so they gathered the marker rocks and stones and
piled them into a barn   they say that the rocks were shaped
some of them scratched with triangles and other forms   they
must have been trying to invent some new language they say
the rocks went to build that wall there guarding the manor and
some few were used for the state house
crops refused to grow
i say the stones marked an old tongue and it was called eternity
and pointed toward the river   i say that after that collection
no pillow in the big house dreamed   i say that somewhere under
here moulders one called alice whose great grandson is old now
too and refuses to talk about slavery   i say that at the
masters table only one plate is set for supper   i say no seed
can flourish on this ground once planted then forsaken   wild
berries warm a field of bones
bloom how you must i say

■

the river between us

in the river that your father fished
my father was baptized.   it was
their hunger that defined them,

one, a man who knew he could
feed himself if it all came down,
the other a man who knew he needed help.

this is about more than color. it is
about how we learn to see ourselves.
it is about geography and memory.

it is about being poor people
in america.   it is about my father
and yours and you and me and
the river that is between us.

■

cancer

the first time the dreaded word
bangs against your eyes so that
you think you must have heard it but
what you know is that the room
is twisting crimson on its hinge
and all the other people there are dolls
watching from their dollhouse chairs

the second time you hear a swoosh as if
your heart has fallen down a well
and shivers in the water there
trying to not drown

the third time and you are so tired
so tired and you nod your head
and smile and walk away from
the angel uniforms the blood
machines and you enter the nearest
movie house and stand in the last aisle
staring at the screen with your living eyes

■

in the mirror

an only breast
leans against her chest wall
mourning   she is suspended
in a sob between t and e and a and r
and the gash ghost of her sister

t and e and a and r

it is pronounced like crying
it is pronounced like
being torn away
it is pronounced like trying to re
member the shape of an unsafe life

■

blood

here in this ordinary house
a girl is pressing a scarf
against her bleeding body
this is happening now

she will continue for over
thirty years emptying and
filling   sistering the moon
on its wild ride

men will march to games and wars
pursuing the bright red scarf
of courage   heroes every moon

some will die   while every moon
blood will enter this ordinary room
this ordinary girl will learn
to live with it

■

a story

for edgar

whose father is that
guarding the bedroom door
watching out for prowling
strangers for beasts and ogres
like in the childrens tale

not yours not mine

ours loomed there in the half
shadow of a daughters room
moaning a lullaby
in a wolfs voice

later
our mothers went mad and
our brothers killed themselves
and we began this storytelling life
wondering whose father that was
wondering how did we survive
to live not happily perhaps but

ever after

■

mercy

how grateful I was when he decided
not to replace his fingers with his thing
though he thought about it was going to
but mumbled "maybe I shouldn't do that"
and didn't do that and I was so
grateful then and now grateful
how sick   i am   how mad

■

here rests

my sister Josephine
born july in '29
and dead these 15 years
who carried a book
on every stroll.

when daddy was dying
she left the streets
and moved back home
to tend him.

her pimp came too
her Diamond Dick
and they would take turns
reading

a bible aloud through the house.
when you poem this
and you will   she would say
remember the Book of Job.

happy birthday and hope
to you Josephine
one of the easts
most wanted.

may heaven be filled
with literate men
may they bed you
with respect.

∎

after oz

midnight we slip into her room
and fill her pockets with stones
so that she is weighted down
so that storms cannot move her

she disappears for hours
then staggers back smelling of straw
of animal

perhaps we have lost her
perhaps home is no longer comfort
or comfort no longer home

evenings we sit awake in
our disenchanted kitchen
listening to the dog whine
to dorothy clicking her heels

■

the Phantom

in his purple mask
his purple body suit
lived with a wolf
called Devil

the village believed him
immortal
the-ghost-who-walks
though he was only a man

i would save up
to go watch him
in his cave of skulls
his penthouse in the city

he would fall in love
with a white girl
like all the heroes
and monsters did

i was a little brown girl

after the show I would
walk home wondering
what would he feel
if he saw me

what is the color of
his country
what is the color
of mine

■

Powell

"i am your worst nightmare"
—black man to white

this is that dream I wake from
crying, then clutch my sleeping wife
and rock her until i fall again
onto a battlefield.   there,
they surround me, nations of darkness
speaking a language i cannot understand
and i suspect that something about
my life they know and hate and i hate them
for knowing it so well.   my son,
i think about my son, my golden daughter,
and as they surround me, nearer, nearer,
i reach to pick up anything,
a tool, a stick, a weapon and
something begins to die.   this
is that dream.

(powell was one of the officers
who beat rodney king.)

■

walking the blind dog

for wsm

          then he walks the blind dog muku
named for the dark of the moon
out to the park where she can smell
the other dogs and hear their
yips their puppy dreams

her one remaining eye is star lit
though it has no sight and
in its bright blue crater
is a vision of the world

old travelers who feel the way from here
to there and back again
who follow through the deep
grass the ruff of breeze
rustling her black coat   his white hair

both of them
poets
trusting the blind road home

■

hands

the snips of finger
fell from the sterile bowl
into my mind and after that
whatever i was taught they would
point toward a different learning
which i followed

i could no more ignore
the totems of my tribe
than i could close my eyes
against the light flaring
behind what has been called
the world

look   hold these regulated hands
against the sky
see how they were born to more
than bone   see how their shadow
steadies what i remain   whole
alive   twelvefingered

■

wind on the st. marys river

january 2002

it is the elders trying to return
sensing the coast is near and they
will soon be home again

they have walked under two oceans
and too many seas
the nap of their silver hair whipping
as the wind sings out to them
this way   this way

and they come rising steadily not
swimming exactly toward shore
toward redemption
but the wind dies down

and they sigh and still and descend
while we watch from our porches
not remembering their names not calling out
Jeremiah   Fanny Lou   Geronimo   but only

white caps on the water   look white caps

■

the tale the shepherds tell the sheep

that some will rise
above shorn clouds of fleece
and some will feel their bodies break
but most will pass through this
into sweet clover
where all   all will be sheltered safe
until the holy shearing
don't think about the days to come
sweet meat
think of my arms
trust me

■

stop

what you are doing
stop
what you are not doing
stop
what you are seeing
stop
what you are not seeing
stop
what you are hearing
stop
what you are not hearing
stop
what you are believing
stop
what you are not believing

in the green hills
of hemingway
nkosi has died
again
and again
and again

stop

—*for Nkosi Johnson*
2/4/89–6/1/01

■

september song
a poem in 7 days

1   tuesday 9/11/01

thunder and lightning and our world
is another place   no day
will ever be the same   no blood
untouched

they know this storm in otherwheres
israel   ireland   palestine
but God has blessed America
we sing

and God has blessed America
to learn that no one is exempt
the world is one   all fear

is one   all life   all death
all one

2   wednesday 9/12/01

this is not the time
i think
to note the terrorist
inside
who threw the brick
into the mosque
this is not the time
to note
the ones who cursed
Gods other name
the ones who threatened
they would fill the streets
with arab children's blood
and this is not the time
i think
to ask who is allowed to be
american   America
all of us gathered under one flag
praying together safely
warmed by the single love
of the many tongued God

3   thursday 9/13/01

the firemen
ascend
like jacobs ladder
into the mouth of
history

4   friday 9/14/01

some of us know
we have never felt safe

all of us   americans
weeping

as some of us have wept
before

is it treason to remember

what have we done
to deserve such villainy

nothing we reassure ourselves
nothing

5   saturday 9/15/01

i know a man who perished for his faith.
others called him infidel, chased him down
and beat him like a dog.   after he died
the world was filled with miracles.
people forgot he was a jew and loved him.
who can know what is intended?   who can understand
the gods?

6   **sunday morning 9/16/01**

for bailey

the st. marys river flows
as if nothing has happened

i watch it with my coffee
afraid and sad as are we all

so many ones to hate and i
cursed with long memory

cursed with the desire to understand
have never been good at hating

now this new granddaughter
born into a violent world

as if nothing has happened

and i am consumed with love
for all of it

the everydayness of bravery
of hate of fear of tragedy

of death and birth and hope
true as this river

and especially with love
bailey fredrica clifton goin

for you

7   monday sundown 9/17/01

Rosh Hashanah

i bear witness to no thing
more human than hate

i bear witness to no thing
more human than love

apples and honey
apples and honey

what is not lost
is paradise

■

the message from The Ones

(received in the late 70s)

beginning of message

your mother sends you this

you have a teapot
others have teapots
if you abuse them
they will break

you have a gift
others have gifts
if you abuse them

you understand

she advises you
you are special to her
she advises you
we are not she

■

come to here
each morning
for a word

we will bring
logos
with us
to this table
this chair

meet us here
each morning   yes

why you
why not

■

you
are not chosen

any stone
can sing

we come
to languages
not lives

your tongue
is useful
not unique

∎

we are ones
who have not rolled
selves into bone and flesh

call us the ones

we will call you
one eye
field of feeling
singing ear
quick hand

we will make use
of these

■

in the saying of
you
we will sometime
be general
and sometime
particular

in the saying of we
we are we

∎

we are here
between the lines

you reach through us
to raise your morning cup

you have assigned us countries
of the dead
but we are neither dead
nor emigrant

we are just here
where you are

■

why should we wander bone yards
draped in linen

flesh is the coat we unfasten
and throw off

what need to linger among stones
and monuments

we have risen away from all that
wrapped in understanding

■

some of you have been blessed
or cursed
to see beyond yourselves

into the scattered wrongful dead
into the disappeared
the despised

none of you has seen
everything
none of you has said
everything

what you have not noticed
we have noticed
what you have ignored
we have not

■

you come to teach
and to learn

you do not know
anothers lesson

pay attention to
what sits inside yourself
and watches you

you may sometime discover
which when
which which

∎

in the geometry
of knowing
we have no new thing
to tell
only the same old
almanac
january
love one another
february
whatever you sow
you will reap

∎

we
who have not been
human
have not learned
to love it
more

human is neither
wiser
nor more blessed

it is not wise
to count oneself
the only servant
of ones lord

it is not wise
to count oneself
the favorite servant
of ones lord

■

god
is
love

no

god
is love
is light
is god

no

place here
the name
you give
to god
is love
is light
is
here the name
you give
to

yes

■

the angels have no wings
they come to you wearing
their own clothes

they have learned to love you
and will keep coming

unless you insist on wings

■

you who feel yourself
drowning in the bodys need
what can you know clearly
of fleshlessness

there is no hunger here
we come to you directly
without touching

you who lie awake
holding your mouth open
receive us as best you can
and we enter you

as we must
tongueless
as best we can

■

you wish to speak of
black and white
no
you wish to hear of
black and white

have we not talked of human

every human comes
to every color
some remember
some do not

■

you are not
your brothers keeper
you are
your brother

the one
hiding in the bush
is you

the one
lying on the grate
is you

the mad one in the cage
or at the podium
is you

the king is you
the kike is you
the honky is you
the nigger is you
the bitch is you
the beauty is you
the friend is you
the enemy   oh

others have come
to say this
it is not
metaphor

you are not
your sisters keeper
you are
your sister   yes

■

the universe requires the worlds
to be
each leaf is veined from the mother/ father
each heart is veined from the mother/ father
each leaf each heart has a place
irreplaceable
each is required to be

■

you have placed yourselves
in peril
not by your superior sword
but by your insignificant
quarrels with life

no   by your quarrels with
insignificant life   yes

there are some languages
some fields some sky
the lord of language field and sky
is lonely for

they have been worlds
they will be worlds again

your world is in grave danger

■

whether in spirit
or out of spirit
we don't know

only that balance
is the law

balance
or be balanced

whether in body
or out of body
we don't know

■

the air
you have polluted
you will breathe

the waters
you have poisoned
you will drink

when you come again
and you will come again

the air
you have polluted
you will breathe

the waters
you have poisoned
you will drink

■

the patience
of the universe
is not without
an end

so might it
slowly
turn its back

so might it
slowly
walk away

leaving you alone
in the world you leave
your children

■

what has been made
can be unmade

saints have begun to enter
wearing breasts
hoping for children
nursed toward wholeness
holiness

it is perhaps
a final chance

not the end of the world
of a world

■

there is a star
more distant
than eden
something there
is even now
preparing

■

end of message

Voices

(2008)

for my little bird
and
my beamish boy

"all goodbye ain't gone"

hearing

"marley was dead to begin with"

from *A Christmas Carol*

then in trenchtown and in babylon
the sound of marleys ghost
rose and began to fill the air
like in the christmas tale

his spirit shuddered and was alive
again   his dreadful locks
thick in the voices of his children

ziggy and i and i marley again
standing and swaying
everything gonna be alright
little darling
no woman   no cry

■

aunt jemima

white folks say i remind them
of home   i who have been homeless
all my life except for their
kitchen cabinets

i who have made the best
of everything
pancakes   batter for chicken
my life

the shelf on which i sit
between the flour and cornmeal
is thick with dreams
oh how i long for

my own syrup
rich as blood
my true nephews   my nieces
my kitchen   my family
my home

■

uncle ben

mother guineas favorite son
knew rice and that was almost
all he knew
not where he was
not why
not who were the pale sons
of a pale moon
who had brought him here
rice   rice   rice
and so he worked the river
worked as if born to it
thinking only now and then
of himself   of the sun
of afrika

■

cream of wheat

sometimes at night
we stroll the market aisles
ben and jemima and me   they
walk in front   remembering this and that
i lag behind
trying to remove my chefs cap
wondering about what ever pictured me
then left me personless
Rastus
i read in an old paper
i was called rastus
but no mother ever
gave that to her son   toward dawn
we return to our shelves
our boxes   ben and jemima and me
we pose and smile   i simmer   what
is my name

■

horse prayer

why was i born to balance
this two-leg
on my back   to carry
across my snout
his stocking of oat and apple
why   i pray to You
Father Of What Runs And Swims
in the name of the fenceless
field   when he declares himself
master
does he not understand my
neigh

■

raccoon prayer

oh Master Of All Who Take And Wash
And Eat   lift me away at the end into evening
forever   into sanctified crumples of paper
and peelings curled over my hand
i have scavenged as i must
among the hairless
now welcome this bandit into the kingdom
just as you made him
barefoot and faithful and clean

■

dog's god

has lifted dog
on four magnificent legs
has blessed him with fur
against the cold
and blessed him with
two-legs to feed him
and clean his waste
gods dog
spins and tumbles
in the passion
of his praise

■

albino

for kathy

we sat
in the stalled
car
watching him
watch us
his great pink
antlers
branched
his pink eyes
fixed
on the joy
of the black woman
and the white one
laughing together
and he smiled
at the sometime
wonderfulness
of other

■

mataoka

(actual name of pocahontas)

in the dream was white men
walking up from the river

in the dream was our land
stolen away and our horses
and our names

in the dream was my father
fighting to save us   in the dream
the pipe was broken

and i was leaning my body
across the whimpering
white man

if our father loves revenge
more than he loves his children
spoke the dream

we need to know it now

∎

witko

aka crazy horse

the man
who wore a blue stone
behind his ear
did not dance
dreamed
clear fields
and redmen everywhere
woke and braided
his curling brown hair
as his enchanted horse
who woke with him
prepared
whispering
Hoka Hay brother
it is a good day
to die

■

what haunts him

that moment after the bartender
refused to serve the dark marine
and the three white skinned others
just sat there   that moment
before they rose and followed
their nappy brother
out into the USA they were
willing to die to defend
then

■

my grandfather's lullaby

pretty little nappy baby
rockin in that chair
theys a world outside
the window
and somebody in it hates you

let me hold you baby
and love you all i can
better to hear it from papa
than learn it all alone

■

"you have been my tried and trusted friend"

said the coal miners son
to the chippers daughter
then turned his head and died
and she and their children rose
and walked behind the coffin
to the freeway
                    after a while
she started looking at
other womens husbands other
womens sons but she had been
tried and trusted once and
though once is never enough
she knew two may be too
many

■

lu
1942

what i know is
this is called gravel
you must not eat it
you must not throw it
at your brother

what i know is
over there is our house
our sidewalk too
there is no grass   grass
is for the white folks section

what i know is
something is coming   mama
calls it war   calls it change
mama loves me   daddy
loves me too much

what i know is
this is in the middle
i am in the middle
come in   come in my mama calls
you can't stay there forever

■

sorrows

who would believe them winged
who would believe they could be

beautiful   who would believe
they could fall so in love with mortals

that they would attach themselves
as scars attach and ride the skin

sometimes we hear them in our dreams
rattling their skulls   clicking

their bony fingers
they have heard me beseeching

as i whispered into my own
cupped hands   enough   not me again

but who can distinguish
one human voice

amid such choruses
of desire

■

being heard

this is what i know
my mother went mad
in my fathers house
for want of tenderness

this is what i know
some womens days
are spooned out
in the kitchen of their lives

this is why i know
the gods
are men

■

my father hasn't come back
to apologize   i have stood
and waited almost sixty years
so different from the nights
i wedged myself between
the mattress and the wall

i do not hate him
i assure myself
only his probing fingers
i have to teach you
he one time whispered
more to himself than me

i am seventy-two-years-old
dead man and in another city
standing with my daughters   granddaughters
trying to understand you
trying to help them understand
the sticks and stones of love

■

dad

consider the raw potato
wrapped in his dress sock
consider his pocket
heavy with loose change
consider his printed list
of whitemens names

for beating her
and leaving no bruises
for bus fare
for going bail
for vouching for him
he would say

consider
he would say
the gods might
understand
a man like me

■

faith

my father was so sure
that afternoon
he put on his Sunday suit
and waited at the front porch
one hand in his pocket
the other gripping his hat
to greet the end of the world

waited there patient as the eclipse
ordained the darkening
of everything
the house   the neighborhood we knew
the world   his hopeful eyes the only
glowing things on purdy street

■

afterblues

"i hate to see the evening sun go down"

my mothers son
died in his sleep

and so did mine
both of them found

though years apart
hands folded in

unexpected prayer
cold on a bed

of trouble   my brother
my son

my mama was right
theys blues
in the night

■

the dead do dream

scattered   they dream of gathering
each perfect ash to each
so that where there was blindness
there is sight
and all the awkward bits
discarded

if they have been folded
into boxes
they dream themselves spilling
out and away
their nails grown long and
menacing

some of them dream they are asleep
on ordinary pillows
they rise to look around
their ordinary rooms
to walk among the lives
of their heedless kin

■

"in 1844 explorers John Fremont
and Kit Carson discovered Lake Tahoe"

—Lodge guidebook

in 1841 Washoe children
swam like otters in the lake
their mothers rinsed red beans
in 1842 Washoe warriors began to dream
dried bones and hollow reeds
they woke clutching their shields
in 1843 Washoe elders began to speak
of grass hunched in fear and
thunder sticks over the mountain
in 1844 Fremont and Carson

■

mirror

one day
we will look into the mirror
and the great nation standing there
will shake its head and frown
they way babies do who
are just born
and cant remember
why they asked for just
these people   just this chance
and when we close our eyes
against regret
we will be left alone
in the wrong image   not understanding
what we are or what we
had hoped to be

■

6/27/06

pittsburgh   you in white
like the ghost
of all my desires   my heart
stopped and renamed itself
i was thirty-six
today i am seventy   my eyes
have dimmed from looking for you
my body has swollen from swallowing
so much love

■

in amira's room

you are not nearly light enough
i whisper to myself
staring up at the stars
on amiras ceiling

you are my lightest grandchild
she would smile
crazy lady who loved me more
of course

shining among my cousins
in my maryjanes
sure that i could one day
lift from the darkness

from the family holding me
to what the world would call
unbearable
i lie here now

under my godchilds ceiling
grandma gone   cousins all gone
the dark world still
smug still visible
among the stars

■

for maude

what i am forgetting doubles everyday
what i am remembering
is you   is us aging
though you called me girl
i can feel us   white haired
nappy and not
listening to marvin
both of us wondering
whats going on   all of us
wondering   oh darlin girl
what   what   what

■

highway 89 toward tahoe

a congregation
of red rocks
sits at attention
watching the water
the trees among them
rustle hosanna
hosanna
something stalls the rental car
something moves us
something in the river
Christ
rowing for our lives

∎

ten oxherding pictures

a meditation on ten oxherding pictures

here are the hands
they are still
if i ask them to rise
they will rise
if i ask them to turn
they will turn in an arc
of perfect understanding
they have allowed me only such
privilege as owed to flesh
or bone   no more   they know
they belong to the ox

■

1st picture
searching for the ox

they have waited my lifetime for this
something has entered the hands
they stir
the fingers come together
caressing each others tips
in a need beyond desire
until the silence has released
something like a name
they move away   i follow
it is the summons from the ox

■

2nd picture
seeing the traces

as tracks
in the buffalo snow
leading to only
a mirror
and what do they make of that
the hands

or baltimore
voices whispering
in a room where no one sits
except myself

and what do the hands make of that

■

3rd picture
seeing the ox

not the flesh
not the image
of the flesh
not the bone
nor the clicking
of the bone
not the brain
wearing its mask
not the mind
nor its disguises
not this me
not that me
now here where
no thing is defined
we are coming to the ox

■

4th picture
catching the ox

i whisper come
and something comes
i am cautioned by the hands

■

5th picture
herding the ox

the hands refuse to gather
they sit in their pockets as i
command ox and enhance my name
i am lucille who masters ox
ox is the one lucille masters
hands caution me again
what can be herded
is not ox

■

6th picture
coming home on the ox's back

i mount the ox
and we shamble
on toward the city together
our name is inflated
as we move   lucille
who has captured ox
ox who supports lucille
we meet a man who wears
authority   he defines ox
describes him
the man claims ox
i claim the man

■

7th picture
the ox forgotten   leaving the man
alone

i have been arriving
fifty years   parents
children lovers
have walked with me
eating me like cake
and i am a good baker
somewhere i was going
fifty years
hands shiver in their pockets
dearly beloved
where is ox

∎

8th picture
the ox and the man both gone
out of sight

man is not ox
i am not ox
no thing is ox
all things are ox

■

9th picture
returning to the origin
back to the source

what comes
when you whisper ox
is not
the ox
ox
begins in silence
and ends
in the folding
of hands

■

10th picture
entering the city
with bliss-bestowing hands

we have come to the gates
of the city
the hands begin to move
i ask of them
only forgiveness
they tremble as they rise

■

end of meditation

what is ox
ox is
what

■

note

Ten Oxherding Pictures is an allegorical series composed as a training guide for Chinese Buddhist monks. The pictures are attributed to kaku-an shi-en, twelfth-century Chinese Zen master. I was unaware of them until after these poems were written. I had only read the titles of the pictures.

■

Uncollected Poems

(2006–2010)

Book of Days
(2006)

birth-day

today we are possible.

the morning, green and laundry-sweet,
opens itself and we enter
blind and mewling.

everything waits for us:

the snow kingdom
sparkling and silent
in its glacial cap,

the cane fields
shining and sweet
in the sun-drenched south.

as the day arrives
with all its clumsy blessings

what we will become
waits in us like an ache.

■

godspeak: out of paradise

what more could you ask than this
good earth, good sky?
you are like mad children
set in a good safe bed
who by morning
will have torn the crib apart
and be howling on a cold floor
among the ruins.

■

lucifer morning-star to man-kind after the fall: in like kind

bright things
winged and unwinged
fall still
through the dark closets of night.

the hand that made them
made you, made me:
the same perfect reckless hand.

will you still insist
you cannot understand
how it is possible to stumble,

one eye filling with darkness,
the other bright with heaven-light,
with its unreachable unbearable glory?

■

man-kind: in image of

we learn what it is to live
inside the enemy's skin:
ashes to ashes, dust to dust,
the spirit lodged in us
like a stone
riding out the difficult light.

■

angelspeak

god keeps himself in a place now
so far above the mortal and immortal worlds
that in order for us to abandon him again
we'd have to hurl ourselves
from such a height that
to survive another fall would be impossible.

■

mother-tongue: the land of nod

true, this isn't paradise
but we come at last to love it

for the sweet hay and the flowers rising,
for the corn lining up row on row,

for the mourning doves who
open the darkness with song,

for warm rains
and forgiving fields,

and for how, each day,
something that loves us

tries to save us.

■

mother-tongue: to the child just born

if i were eloquent in your language
i would try to tell you

how it is
when something difficult loves you,

how it is
when you begin to love it back,

how this can
cost you everything.

■

mother-tongue: after the child's death

tell me this one thing, god:
in which room of the heart
is the fortress,
is the inside wall that saves you?

■

mother-tongue: after the flood

the rain repeats its story
until we have it by heart,
always the same.

lord, in between
the solitudes of birth and death
the solitudes of life
will almost do us in.

■

the rainbow bears witness

you will see him one day just as you see me:
hung between earth and heaven,
unwilling to relinquish one for the other,
held fast in the swift glory,
in the bittersweet martyrdom of love.

■

nineveh: waiting

everything here will grow ocean-wise,
even the man, sea-wall strong,
here where Leviathan
will spit him out one day:
a half-dead, luke-warm thing.

though he will turn inland
away from the terrible journey,
away from this unloved city,
he will find that even its memory

will cling, like salt,
to every thing.

■

mother-tongue: babylon

our children will not remember a place
where the wind does not sleep at night like this,
at ease in the arms of trees.
they will know no waters
more lovely than these
where we, in our exile, weep.

though we are lovely,
we suffer from such loneliness,
the way even these moonlit waters would suffer
if only the blind stars looked on
night after night after night.

who could bear for long
the weight of such beauty as this?

■

mother-tongue: to man-kind

all that i am asking is
that you see me as something
more than a common occurrence,
more than a woman in her ordinary skin.

■

godspeak

little ones,
small and treacherous,
why would you believe that *I* punish you
who punish each other relentlessly
and with such enthusiasm?

■

mother-tongue: we are dying

no failure in us
that we can be hurt like this,
that we can be torn.

death is a small stone
from the mountain we were born to.

we put it in a pocket
and carry it with us
to help us find our way home.

■

mother-tongue: in a dream before she died

jesus was in the living room
wearing her blue housecoat.

he raised the blinds
to let the morning in.

then he went to the door
and freed the parakeet.

the last thing he did
before he left was to turn

all her fresh-baked bread
back to stones.

■

sodom and gomorrah

1.   *what was*

mirror-images:
twin cities like two bodies
blasted in a single furnace

2.   *what is*

drawn here by the after-burn of light,
they are too frail in sin
to be any good at it:

the men drowning
in the darkness of their own hearts,
in the weight of commandments
that broke at the ends of their fingers

and the women
like wronged angels and
fallen things: no children
will hold in the cyanide nests of their bodies.

3.   *what waits*

house of the rope
house of the razor
temple of bullets and pills:

the bright doors line up
and the knowing stars
ride out the whole incendiary night.

■

prodigal

illusion is
your prettiest trick.

free will, you said.

but all the roads
that seemed to lead away
have circled back again to you,
old father, old necessity.

■

man-kind: over the jordan, into the promised land

all those years in a cold river,
treading water,
only to set foot on dry land again
and find nothing waiting here for me,
only to find milk and honey
screaming at me
from the *other* side.

■

lucifer morning-star

the wings are myth:
had i wings
i would have flown by now.

what i have are feet
that never carry me where i need to be
and a road that does not go
all the way in any direction.

time is what is left to me,
the one immortal angel always falling
far from the glory gallows
and the resurrection.

■

armageddon

i am all that will be
left to them in that day.

men will come here, full armed,
to make their last war.

their bodies will
litter this valley floor.

they will lie here together then,
intimate and quiet as lovers,

their ruby hearts still bleeding through in places.

■

man-kind: digging a trench to hell

did i go deep enough?

i've exhausted the earth,
the plentiful garden,
the woman,
myself.

i've exhausted even the darkness now.

are you not done with me yet?

■

godspeak: kingdom come

you, with your point-blank fury,
what if i told you
this is all there ever was:
this earth, this garden, this woman,
this one precious, perishable kingdom.

■

Last Poems & Drafts
(2006–2010)

6/27/06
seventy

my bones are ice
there is a blizzard here

my memories are frozen
sharp with loneliness

every hair of my body
has turned to snow

my mother never spoke of this

she died at forty-four
leaving me to wonder

who loses   who wins

■

some points along some of the meridians

heart

spirit path
spirit gate
blue green spirit
little rushing in
utmost source
little storehouse

lung

very great opening
crooked marsh
cloud gate
middle palace

stomach

receive tears
great welcome
people welcome
heavenly pivot
earth motivator
abundant splendor
inner courtyard

liver

walk between
great esteem
happy calm
gate of hope

kidney

bubbling spring
water spring
great mountain stream
deep valley
spirit storehouse
spirit seal
spirit burial ground
chi cottage

large intestine

joining of the valleys
1st interval
2nd interval
heavenly shoulder bone
welcome of a glance

spleen

supreme light
great enveloping
encircling glory
sea of blood
3 yin crossing

gates

stone gate
gate of life
inner frontier gate
outer frontier gate

∎

untitled

and if i could name this
in a frenzy of understanding
it would be called hunger
that sits in a womans spaces
and it would be called need
that bleeds into the bones
and it would be called bowl
that cannot be filled and
heart melting into never and
no and yes and and

■

she leans out from the mirror,
big-breasted woman
with skinny legs. "Put this
into your poems," she grimaces,
raising her gown above her head.
and there is nothing there, not
the shadow of paradise even,
only the empty glass and the   echo
of bitch   bitch bitch.

■

Titled

and stamped and approved
so that we fit into the file
the world understands but in
the spaces between the lines
there is printed, "poet,
no blame, no name, no why."

■

new orleans

when the body floated by me
on the river   it was a baby
body thin and brown
it was not my alexandra
my noah
not even my river
it was a dream
but when i woke i knew
somewhere there is a space
in a grandmother's sleep
if she can sleep
if she is alive
and i want her to know
that the baby is not abandoned
is in grandmothers hearts
and we will remember
forever

■

after the children died she started bathing
only once in a while
started spraying herself with ginger
trying to preserve what remained of her heart

but the body insists on truth.
she did not want to be clean
in such a difficult world
but there were other children

and she would not want me
to tell you this

■

haiku

over the mountains
and under the stars   it is
one hell of a ride

■

An American Story

one year
a naked white guy
parked his car
by our elementary school
kids called him
The Nude Dude and laughed
when they told the story
i didn't believe it
because i was
on the honor roll
until the afternoon
he hopped at me
all pink and sweaty
and asked me
                little girl
have you ever seen
a white mans pride
and i replied oh
yes sir many times
many times

■

God Bless America

You don't know the half of it, like the old folks used to say
but the half of it is what I do know
What I don't know is the other

■

In the middle of the Eye,
not knowing whether to call it
devil or God
I asked how to be brave
and the thunder answered,
"Stand. Accept." so I stood
and I stood and withstood
the fiery sight.

■

won't you celebrate with me:
the poetry of Lucille Clifton

National Book Award winner, Fellow of the Academy of Arts and Sciences, Chancellor of the Academy of American Poets, children's books author, mother, memoirist, *Jeopardy* champion, survivor, poet, and national treasure, Lucille Clifton was at the height of her poetic powers when she died in February 2010.

Clifton's work is phenomenally varied, and simultaneously of the moment—fresh and forward-seeking. In tracing the roots (and telling the tales) of a black family, her memoir *Generations* was groundbreaking and could be said to forecast the rise in the attention paid to black genealogy. But Clifton's work also critiques family and country, mourns and makes known what one book of hers calls "the terrible stories." She's as interested in soul as body, her poetry paying "homage to my hips" and providing "wishes for sons"; biblical in her lines as Whitman, she invites an American "I," this time lowercase.

To mention Clifton's winning *Jeopardy* is not to say that Clifton is interested in trivia, but rather, in knowledge. (The win is something she was quite proud of—as well the set of encyclopedias that came with it.) As you'll recall, the *Jeopardy* game show provides the answers and contestants (and we at home) provide the questions; in her work, Clifton's questioning of ourselves adds up to an answer, and in her answering our need for history or pride or praise she also asks a lot of us, too.

At a Poetry Society of America event honoring her in 2004, I called Clifton our Neruda, and I still think this is accurate: like him, she's interested in the large issues, the human ones, and does them justice in a literal sense. I was going to say that she does so through small things, but looking over her work of nearly fifty years there's nothing small but the lack of capital letters; instead we have dreams and shapeshifters and elegy and many kinds of visitation, whether from a fox or "the Ones." Like poet Ted Hughes, she writes of animal and spirit and any number of spirit animals, including "raccoon prayers" and even "yeti poets." Like Neruda, she writes of love, politics, loneliness, and justice.

She also, like Neruda, crafts odes to her elements (cooking greens), the body (hair, hips), and a large-scale idea of America. One of these includes what it means to be a black woman, something she names, implies, connects with, and calls out from—often to her fellow women poets, from Gwendolyn Brooks to Margaret Walker to Maxine Kumin. It is no wonder that one of her earliest poems, from the 1950s, is "To E.D."—Emily Dickinson, whose short lines and unique punctuation, or lack thereof, she would seem to, as we say, call kin.

Clifton too should be considered alongside the same company she kept when the *New York Times* cited her first book among the twenty best books of 1969. As the only woman (and poet) in the "fiction" category, Clifton appears alongside *Portnoy's Complaint* by Philip Roth, *Pricksongs and Descants* by Robert Coover, *Slaughterhouse-Five* by Kurt Vonnegut, John Fowles's *The French Lieutenant's Woman*, and even *The Godfather* by Mario Puzo. (It was a notable year.) Much like these, Clifton's debut endures as a modern classic.

In Clifton's hands, the ordinary, including even punctuation, is transformed—like Superman, who figures in some of her poems, she leaps and soars, crossing bridges as one poem has it, "between starshine and clay." She is also a poet often engaged with the mystic, whether in the form of dream or the "two-headed woman," soothsayer and homemade prophet. Her unique perspective is reflected in the ways she talks about, and often speaks for, the family, often in its most invisible arenas—from "the lost baby poem" to evictions, to her regular reflections on her birthday and other significant, life-changing dates. It is no wonder that she would write a suite of public poems after September 11th. If Whitman's poetic self contained a multitude, often through the metaphor of a burgeoning nation, Clifton's poetic self embraces its multitude through the metaphor of family.

born in babylon: *Early Uncollected Poems, 1965–1969*

The early, previously unpublished work of Lucille Clifton is remarkable for its clarity. As in the selection found here, we can see in the early work many of the themes of her mature work, noting the ways that, even starting out, Clifton established a unique, consistent perspective. Before her first book, we can see her distinctive voice: a poem like "Black Women," which opens the section, reveals not only many of her concerns but also her effective use of the line, its music in its nascent form and suggestive of her future development.

The poems in this first section are found in her archive at Emory University's Manuscript, Archives, and Rare Book Library (MARBL) in a folder she labeled "UNPUBLISHED POEMS." This type has been crossed out sometime later, replaced with her handwritten note: "Old Poems and Ones that May Not Be Poems at all and Maybe should be thrown away One Day"; and then at another point, simply "Bad Poems." There are some who would say that the mere presence of such phrases confirms these are "not poems at all" and should indeed be thrown away—to do otherwise is to violate the writer's wishes, never mind whenever they were made. There are some who would urge us to have burned Kafka's work, hewing to his instructions after his death, no matter the cost to literature.

But we already have seen such burning of poems by Clifton's own mother. In a story she would recount both in writing and in person, Clifton's mother wrote poems—after her husband, Clifton's father, disapproved of them, Ruby Sayles set fire to her own work, spiting both her husband and herself. Clifton reads this act of self-immolation as a cautionary tale: one that instructs on the limits too often placed on black female imagination; and on the cost of not saying so, the dear price of silence. She is writing poems for a mother whose own life and poems were taken away, too soon and forever.

Clifton protests, questions, and crafts her mother's self-defeating defiance into a rallying cry for her verse. To not include these early yet mature poems she saved despite her shifting labels would seem to ignore such a cry, what later she would call, speaking metaphorically about a fox that visits her, "the poet in her, the poet and / the terrible stories she could tell." These formerly unpublished poems seem to us—and one suspects, to a Clifton who saved them—"bad" only in that sense of the "terrible stories" they tell. They are terrific in both senses.

What's more, those who knew and loved Clifton well knew she had no problem discarding work. Indeed, she must have done so regularly, as little work from before the 1960s survives; nor do we have any drafts of the poems in her first book, *Good Woman* (1969), though we do have versions of its typescripts. It appears at least early on, whenever a poem was finished, Clifton's practice was to destroy her drafts, letting the last version stand.

Fortunately for us, there are a small number of notebook-page poems, written in a delicate penmanship—one of which is dated 1955—that might be best described as juvenilia, complete with rhyme and inverted archaic phrasing. In other words, nothing like the fifty-some poems in the "Bad Poems" folder, which are rather clean, free from handwritten edits, many even prepared and addressed for submission to magazines. It is clear these previously unpublished poems are ones she worked and reworked: we can see her testing out lines, even recasting them (as she does in "Black Women") in another poem ("Conversation Overheard in a Graveyard"); on a few occasions she rewrites poems entirely, or subtly (as revealed in the two versions of what one version titles "Miss Ann," slang for the slave mistress). We have tried to represent the range of this work, its depth and also its vitality: "something / like alive." As such, we have let the typography of these uncollected gems stand, down to the titles, in order to give a sense of their varied origins. I have begun to think of these as "Bad Poems" in the vernacular sense, bad meaning good—they are revelations of the poet Clifton already is, and predict the powerful poet she would become.

Dating of these poems is more an art than a science: though she rarely dated any poems, the earliest date we have on a draft is found on "Old Hundred," from 1965. Comparing paper and type, not to mention style, I have placed the poems in a rough chronology. With it, we can see her move from more "public" poems in a broad voice to more personal and, dare I say, profound work, including the remarkable set of Mama "letters" and poems about family—themes that she'd return to and that distinguish her work even early on. Here, in their proper, early context, we can see Clifton work toward the poems that make up her remarkable first book.

Recalling the context of the times makes these poems all the more astonishing. Both the poetry world and the world of the 1960s were in upheaval; the years from 1965 to 1969 saw the assassinations of Malcolm X and Martin Luther King, and the first human walking on the moon, all of which appear in the poems. There was also a revolution in poetry, especially black poetry, which accompanied, described, and descried the unrest in the streets. The Black Arts movement, which Lucille Clifton found herself a part of and in many ways helped to forge, insisted on poems for and about black folks, establishing a black aesthetic based on varying ways of black speech, African structures, and political action.

In such a context, Clifton's "Black Women" poem is a breakthrough, but a shared one. Black Arts sought many things but above all a public poetry—one aware of its audience and even pitched at times toward a newfound audience that it was both meeting and making. Clifton's lasting innovation, which may seem obvious only in retrospect, can be glimpsed in this early work: she would move from a public poetry to a more personal one, crafting poems in sequence that consist of "letters" from Mama, poems to a father and "old hoodoo man" she later will term "old liar old lecher," and poems bridging the divide of racial lines.

By the end of the decade, if Clifton often speaks for a "we," she is also establishing the intimate "I"—soon rendered as a lowercase "i"—that would infuse her work.

both nonwhite and woman: *Good Woman, 1969–1980*

It is with *Good Times* that Clifton's poetry would appear to the world in 1969, naming the turbulent times in a way few would. The book's title contains all Clifton's optimism and irony. In doing so, Clifton counters any predictable kinds of protest, while also offering a group of poems—without any sections, notably interconnected—that take us on a narrative of family as a form of nation. As in her early poems, Clifton finds the site of both protest and possibility in the family: "oh children think about the / good times." Clifton suggests that a poem can and should be made of this daily survival as a kind of celebration. In this way, her title poem is a blues.

Clifton shifts the focus of poetry from the streets to the stoop, from worrying about "the Man" to writing about the family—and what once was called "the family of man." The talk of the poem is just as important as its form, which is also musical, repetitive, spoken; we have here "admonitions":

> boys
> i don't promise you nothing
> but this
> what you pawn
> i will redeem
> what you steal
> i will conceal
> my private silence to
> your public guilt
> is all i got

Interestingly, the original edition has some uppercasing, mostly of proper nouns—and even, occasionally, the "i." (This would be regularized in later versions, edits honored in this volume.) An early carbon also indicates that *Good Times* was once known as "New Thing," proposed with "Illustrations by Sidney, Fredrica, and Channing Clifton," three of her six children. Such a "New Thing" (capitalized) is not simply that found in the poem "if i stand in my window"—in which the poet presses "breasts / against my windowpane / like black birds pushing against glass / because i am somebody / in a New Thing"—but was also a term used by black folks in the know to mean avant-garde jazz. The freedom the poem seeks is similar to that of free jazz—and may be read just as politically as the "new thing" was.

Mostly because they are as much music as polemic, much like fellow poet Michael S. Harper's first book from the following year, the poems and politics of Clifton's debut still resonate, concerned with humanity in the face of the hurricane.

The words "good" and "woman" recur throughout the titles of Clifton's first four books, indicating their shared concerns. Her individual book titles seem not just to conjugate but conjure such words up: *Good Times* (1969), *Good News About the Earth* (1972), *An Ordinary Woman* (1974), and *Two-Headed Woman* (1980), create a kind of extraordinary long poem that Clifton would later gather—along with her memoir *Generations*—in the collection titled *Good Woman*. Clifton's "good woman" is the "poor girl" of Bessie Smith's blues grown up, triumphant.

This *Good Woman* sequence of books marks a remarkable epic of the everyday, including several key sequences that still seem as vital as when they were written. Like its predecessor, *Good News About the Earth* gives "good news" in a time of bad, echoing both the headlines and the black spiritual "Ain't That Good News"; the book also elucidates a more typical Black Arts pantheon of heroes than *Good Times*, from poems "to bobby seale" and "for my sisters." (A set of proofs among her literary papers indicate the book was once termed "Good News About the Earth and Other Heroes" before contracting to simply "Good News" and then to its final form.) The volume starts with a poem "after kent state," where the shooting of peaceful anti-war protesters by National Guardsmen marked a terrifying transformation in the national psyche. Clifton also reads the event along racial lines, despairing that "white ways are / the way of death." Clearly Kent State and the difficulties of the 1960s affected Clifton's work as much as it did the national self-perception.

Despite the title, these are often angry poems—she is giving us good news about "the earth," after all, which isn't the same as about race relations, the United States, or the state of things. Rather, she draws power from what some might call an ecopoetics:

> being property once myself
> i have a feeling for it,
> that's why i can talk
> about environment.
> what wants to be a tree,
> ought to be he can be it.
> same thing for other things.
> same thing for men.

This sense of "the earth" is one that would and will transform throughout her work, furthering and challenging her concerns.

But this is only one part of *Good News*—for the book ends with the remarkable sequence "some jesus." This series of poems in the voice of biblical figures does what mere protest often cannot: it provides a radical perspective made new by the poet imagining an inner life of the saints. (The poems also suggest divinity for the "heroes" of the second section by that name, a not unfamiliar narrative for the martyrs of the civil rights struggle.) Her "calling of the disciples," from Adam and Eve to Lazarus, suggests not only hope but a kind of liberation theology, ending with a "spring song" in which "the world is turning / in the body of Jesus and / the future is possible." Hers is a deity in the mode of Santería or James Weldon Johnson's "The Creation"—a personal, prophetic God who speaks in a black idiom. Hers is a Black Madonna, a mother with womanist concerns.

Such concerns would soon find their way in poems about birth and death, "lucy and her girls." She would express this in *An Ordinary Woman* in poems addressing "the black God, Kali, / a woman God and terrible / with her skulls and breasts." Such a God both simultaneously combats the "Gods" of white Christianity questioned in her poem about the "New Thing," but also embraced by "some jesus." Clifton's "i" contains a multicultural multitude. At the same time, her claim in the book is just to be "ordinary," something bolder than declaring black folks are kings and queens. Such ordinariness is triumphant and transformable: *An Ordinary Woman* is a book of "bones" and "roots," of roaches and her thirty-eighth year. It is a book approaching what some might call midlife, the poet meditating on possibly outliving her mother, who died at forty-four. This early death and loss is an anniversary her poems constantly circle.

Clifton often writes poems of anniversary and commemoration, especially around the anniversary of her own birth. We can see this even in her early work, as in "the poet at thirty two." At the risk of interrupting the sequence of Clifton's books we consider sacred, we have included here a small number of such occasional poems found in her papers or given to friends, placing them in the chronology of the *Collected*. Several are from a manuscript that seems to have been dispersed after *Ordinary Woman*, or have been subsumed by later projects—perhaps explaining the timeframe and transformation between the woman as "ordinary" and "two-headed."

With *Ordinary Woman*, Clifton is not so much a poet of elegy or public memorial as of loss anticipated, remembered, refused:

> in the thirty eighth
> year of my life,
> surrounded by life,
> a perfect picture of
> blackness blessed,
> i had not expected this
> loneliness.

What a sense of upending expectations of blackness and blessedness—rhyming with "loneliness" instead. There is, as in the sound of Charlie Parker's horn, the plaintiveness of John Coltrane, the blues of Bessie and Billie—all the heroes of Black Arts, "blessed" but dying young—an almost overwhelming yearning. Rather than refer to, or merely describe this yearning, the repetition and chorusing of Clifton's poems earn and enact it. If Dante's epic begins "in the middle of life," Clifton's epic pauses there—fearing the tale will remain in an ordinary purgatory.

For Clifton's title *Ordinary Woman* is both a wish and wishful thinking: to be "ordinary" is a respite and a calling, is a way of staking a daily poetry, but also a poetry that brings the extraordinary within grasp. The book ends with an evocation of the poet as "lucy one-eye," the nickname itself a prophet's:

> i was born in a hotel,
> a maskmaker.
> my bones were knit by
> a perilous knife.
> my skin turned around
> at midnight and
> i entered the earth in
> a woman jar.
> i learned the world all
> wormside up
> and this is my yes
> my strong fingers;
> i was born in a bed of
> good lessons
> and it has made me
> wise.

As a maskmaker, the poet is herself perilous, filled with yes and with strong fingers, all which she will name further in her next book.

With *Two-Headed Woman*, Clifton finds herself at the height of her powers—and makes such powers literal. The "some jesus" sequence—like the informal one before it in *Good Times* that evoked kinfolk "tyrone" and "willie b"; like the early "Mama" poems—establishes an "i" that is as American as it is eternal, as biblical as it is black. From here forward, Clifton's books, while made up of individual poems—many of them showstoppers—would also include discrete and informal sequences, often about the world of spirit. *Two-Headed Woman* would return to Biblical settings, evoking Mary as well as a tremendous series "to the blind" and "to the lame." By aligning with such figures as those in need of mercy and the traditional Christian mother of mercy, Clifton evoked not just an "environment" but a humanity that needed voicing.

Taken together, Clifton's spiritual poems, crossing her entire poetic life—and even its afterlife, included here—form a sustained devotional of remarkable clarity and complexity. The result is reminiscent of the work of her friend and fellow poet Denise Levertov and the Unholy Sonnets of Gerard Manley Hopkins (whom Levertov wrote on), not to mention *The Temple* of metaphysical poet George Herbert. To my eye, her lowercase litanies and questioning catechisms remain as shaped and sprung as her predecessors who saw the radical forms of their verse enacting the challenges of faith.

Facing such a challenge, Clifton's personal pantheon would give way to a myth of self. *Two-Headed Woman* finds a metaphor for what might be called Clifton's womanism, or black feminism, but also for the poet herself. The "two-headed woman" is that conjure woman of legend and tradition, the hoodoo practitioner not to be trusted but to be admired and even feared; she is the artist incarnate, filled with secrets which she also reveals and revels in. A still-uncollected poem, "the two headed woman blues," found in her papers (but not this volume) makes this connection perhaps too explicit between the conjure woman and the blues:

> her four eyes notice
> in all directions.
> her ears overhear
> what she's not listening for.

For Clifton, such power is not just folklore, but is embodied in the fact of her being born polydactyl, with twelve fingers. This "witchy" birth both marks and connects her to the other women in her family, including her mother, born with this genetic trait. Extra fingers are a sign of Clifton being an artist, but also of loss; the poet recasts the myth of being "born in a hotel"—a place, like the crossroads, of transition and mythic transfer—with the fact of being "born with twelve fingers." One makes a legend of the self; the other makes the fact of the self into a legend. *Two-Headed Woman* is autobiography as epic.

We might remember too that a "dactyl" is a form of a poetic line (whose name from the Greek means "finger") with one stressed syllable, followed by two unstressed (or "short") ones. While not strictly syllabic, Clifton's verse at this time has a many-fingered music:

> i was born with twelve fingers
> like my mother and my daughter.
> each of us
> born wearing strange black gloves
> extra baby fingers hanging over the sides of our cribs and
> dipping into the milk.
> somebody was afraid we would learn to cast spells
> and our wonders were cut off
> but they didn't understand
> the powerful memories of ghosts.   now
> we take what we want
> with invisible fingers
> and we connect
> my dead mother   my live daughter   and me
> through our terrible shadowy hands.

These "shadowy hands" are also the shadow book of her mother, long ago sacrificed. They also contrast with the body Clifton praises in classic poems like "homage to my hips" and "homage to my hair." These poems of praise are both funny and serious, shadowy and showy.

After *Good News* and *An Ordinary Woman* came *Generations* (1976), Clifton's memoir of her family. Edited by Toni Morrison, the memoir also evokes the "Dahomey woman" of her grandmother, crafting yet another tradition her book inhabits. Clifton would gather *Generations*, along with her first four poetry books, in *Good Woman: Poems and a Memoir 1969–1980*, effectively ending the first phase of her mature writing. One-eyed, two-headed, twelve-fingered, Dahomean, and good—even when she's bad—this woman is a creation as remarkable as Whitman's American "I," ordinary in her extraordinariness and extraordinary in what she calls and makes ordinary.

what did i see to be except myself?: *blessing the boats, 1988–2000*

What would be next for Clifton, appearing the same year as *Good Woman*, was a book aptly titled *Next* (1987). Starting with a section declaring "we are all next," the book is filled with an array of "us": Crazy Horse and "history," leukemia and shapeshifter poems. A sequence of dreams record an array of ancestry, philosophy, and even "my dream about being white." The poems also reckon with "the death of fred clifton," her husband who passed from cancer in 1984 at the age of 49. Just as her mother speaks in one poem about her own death, reminiscent of dream, her late husband speaks from beyond:

> there was all around not the
> shapes of things
> but oh, at last, the things
> themselves.

This is not just a description of the afterlife, but the life Clifton's poems seek. It is a poetic life—and line—that takes William Carlos Williams's "no ideas but in things" and heads inward, and upward.

In a confessional era, *Next* is made up not of confessions so much as dreamscapes, a strategy which paradoxically turns them not less real but more immediate, haunting. Clifton writes of enduring and surviving cancer herself, leukemia transforming into "dream/ritual," "white rabbit," and even in one unrealized poem found in the archive, "leukemia as race." Poems also invoke the "shapeshifter," a menacing male presence suggestive of abuse. No wonder then the body is the seat of struggle and praise. What's more, for Clifton there's no split between the body, the spirit, and the intellect: no ideas but in the body.

Next was followed by *Quilting* (1991), a book that took the title's "women's work" as its galvanizing force, sharing the quilters' communal strength and sophisticated structures. In the title poem, Clifton makes quilting a female inheritance that's part of an "unknown world" too often ignored; the book is not mere complaint, but a reckoning with "wild blessings." There are poems "in praise of menstruation," "to my uterus," "to my last period": "well girl, goodbye, / after thirty-eight

years." One of my favorites is "wishes for sons," both a blessing and
a curse:

> i wish them cramps.
> i wish them a strange town
> and the last tampon.
> i wish them no 7-11.
>
> i wish them one week early
> and wearing a white skirt.
> i wish them one week late.

I've read from and taught this poem a number of times and am always
struck by its generosity and humor, something we can lose sight of given
Clifton's directness, her bravery in saying the unsaid. There's also a
temptation to overlook the sophistication of her craft, whether in the
pacing or the deadpan lines, not to mention the thoughtful paradoxes
(and double negatives) of the poem's end:

> let them think they have accepted
> arrogance in the universe,
> then bring them to gynecologists
> not unlike themselves.

In Clifton's hands, the double negatives add up to a wild blessing.

With her next book, *Book of Light* (1993), Clifton's first name is
again something she writes about and through. Lucille means "light,"
something she earlier evokes in the poem "the light that came to lucille
clifton" (which once had been the title of the whole of *Two-Headed
Woman*). Such a light involves the visitations for ill and good that she
evokes often in her work, from a "yeti poet" to Superman to "leda"
poems that evoke abuse at the hands of a father. These poems evoke
some of *The Terrible Stories* (1996) that would name her next volume,
where the visitation would be from a fox she called a fellow poet.

Like Ted Hughes, Clifton had always used the mystic just beyond
what's seen to frame and inform poems; like Hughes, this poetic regu-

larly involved a shifting set of totemic animals. Where for Hughes the fox and the crow were emblems of myth, the fox that first visits in *The Terrible Stories* is more like "the light that came to lucille clifton"—a nightly visitation that's a version of the poet. Fox is also decidedly a female figure, much the way Clifton genders the moon:

> the moon understands dark places.
> the moon has secrets of her own.
> she holds what light she can.

These visitations continue to illuminate a path both in her poetry and private life that she would not fully reveal to readers until later on.

Though she had been the first person to be a finalist for the Pulitzer Prize for two books in the same year (for *Good Woman* and *Next*) and had been finalist for the National Book Award (for *The Terrible Stories*), Lucille Clifton finally won the National Book Award for *Blessing the Boats: New and Selected Poems 1988–2000*. This was a great acknowledgment of the path she had been clearing in books gathered since *Good Woman*, but also of the new poems of *Blessing*. Many suggest her physical frailty, and there is a sorrow found in the lines, a shade less defiant: "i am tired of understanding."

The self in *Blessing*'s new poems is weary, but also brave; a poem like "donor" addresses the kidney transplant Clifton received from her daughter, but not without telling a story on the self addressed to the daughter, admitting to "trying not to have you." The body, ever-present in Clifton, is here less triumphant, but no less truthful or admirable. There is a "praise song" but it is to an aunt saved from suicide; there are protests of lynching, not in the past but in present-day Texas. These are poems of blessing, in other words, as only Clifton can craft. In her powerful phrase, the poems announce "grief for what is born human, / grief for what is not."

The poems also invoke mortality, often through its opposite: heaven figures here, and paradise, including the exiled Lucifer (whose name she well knows, means "light" too). But perhaps the most fitting figure in *Blessing* is Lazarus, whose resurrection from the dead seems a metaphor for transcending sickness and sorrow, while recognizing both. As the title poem wishes, "may you in your innocence / sail through this to that" while Lazarus says "on the third day i contemplate / what i was moving from / what i was moving toward." This or that, from or toward, the poems wonder—and wander as only a true poet can, filled with Keatsian negative capability—Clifton's kind of double negatives urging us forward.

No wonder her next book would be called *Mercy*.

bridge between starshine and clay: *2000–2010*

In the late 1970s Clifton received a series of messages from the spirit world, examples of what is sometimes called "spirit writing" and Clifton herself occasionally referred to as "automatic writing." Such writings place Clifton squarely in a tradition of prophecy, from Jeremiah to two-headed women, as well as in that fellowship of poets who directly engage the spirit world in their writings. Modern English-language poets from Yeats to Robert Duncan have used spiritualism as generative structures; James Merrill even used the Ouija board to organize his modern epic. Around the same time as Merrill, Clifton received "the message from The Ones"—or The Ones conjured her up—crafting a spiritual epic alongside her poetic one.

Such spirit writing, amounting to four fascinating boxes at Emory University's MARBL, testify to a multitude of often daily sessions for recording these messages. If spirituality had always been on her mind and in her poetry, here it became manifest. Much like the uncollected early work, Clifton seems to have admired this work—she certainly does not seem ashamed of it, but one imagines she wasn't sure what exactly to do with it. With *Mercy* in 2004, Clifton finally transcribed some aspects of "the messages" and allowed them to be published as the final section of the book.

Not quite a poem, or at least one we might think of only from her, these poems channel a prophetic and otherworldly voice, quite literally:

you are not
your brothers keeper
you are
your brother

The result is a poetry that is both hers and not hers, one that may remind us of old forms, both the oral form of folklore and that old, sung, lyric art, the psalm. They seem to me also in a continuum with the selfsame mystical African American traditions that titled *Two-Headed Woman* but also broader senses of motherwit and the searching spirituality of Jean Toomer, who after his *Cane* would write a significant set of *Essentials*, or aphorisms, not to mention his searching, mystical poem, "Blue Meridian." Her effort also evokes William Blake, whose work she recalls in her poem "blake" from *The Terrible Stories*:

saw them glittering in the trees,
their quills erect among the leaves,
angels everywhere. we need new words
for what this is, this hunger entering our
loneliness like birds, stunning our eyes into rays
of hope. we need the flutter that can save
us, something that will swirl across the face
of what we have become and bring us grace.
back north, i sit again in my own home
dreaming of blake, searching the branches
for just one poem.

With *Mercy*, Clifton writes what she fears may be "last words," titling poems "cancer" and "after oz"; she is writing too after September 11th, which appears in the sequence "september song." Mercy is what the poems seek and show us, dedicated to her two children who passed away in 2000 and 2004: "the only mercy is memory." *Mercy* also manages to be a book of Clifton's present, despite what might in other hands be pure elegy. Is the poet wrestling with mortality? Are The Ones welcoming the poet into an afterlife, or an other world Clifton clearly saw as nearer and less faraway than others might?

Part of the power of Clifton's late work comes from how contemplative yet forward-looking it is. With *Voices* (2008), the last full-length book published in her lifetime, Clifton returned to questions of race with a newfound grace and humor. (She told me once she considered calling the collection *Colored Girls*.) Figures like "aunt jemima" and "uncle ben" became part of her pantheon; by taking on pop culture, Clifton did not abandon the totemic world of Yeti and The Ones, instead offering a "raccoon prayer" and revisiting Crazy Horse under his original name, Witko.

What Clifton seeks is a community—one we realize she has been crafting all along, making family members myths and myths familiar and familial. She warns us against holding such myths too dear—or rather, "aunt jemima" does, when she speaks—but Clifton also manages an intimacy suggested by her section titles, "hearing" and "being heard." The last section contains "ten oxherding pictures," a sequence Clifton first published in a fine press limited edition in 1988. This work in many ways does what The Ones did for the other volume, consolidating and communicating with another tradition, here Buddhist. Her multitudes keep multiplying.

If we ended with *Mercy* and *Voices*, that would perhaps be enough—they are poems of benediction in a sense, aware of mortality, and aware of our constant longing for more. We are fortunate however that the poet seems to have left behind the start of a manuscript, "Book of Days," that extends her reach and wishes even further.

It is a book that almost did not survive. My fellow editor, Michael S. Glaser, worked with Clifton at St. Mary's in Maryland for years; when she cleaned out her office after retiring in 2006, she threw away a number of things, including poems, many in her hand or with her clear edits—all of which are now part of her archive (and reprinted here in "Last Poems & Drafts"). The typescript for "Book of Days" was among these discards, complete it seems, without any editorial markings or even her name. (This is not unusual: we can almost judge a poem as hers among her papers because it doesn't bear her name.) As I mentioned, Clifton was perfectly capable of tossing away her own poems, even good ones; I myself rescued a few from the maw of the trash. Perhaps she felt there were often other copies on her computer? Fortunately for us Glaser resurrected "Book of Days"—a title Clifton's daughter Alexia recalls her working on—for the sequence is a wonder, a manuscript that seems quite complete, mournful yet mindful, concerned with birth, death, and that "what we will become / waits in us like an ache." These new poems, found in 2006, seem to be ones that extend her concerns and provide an alternate ending to what she herself lived to publish. If it indeed is what it appears to be, this is a poet in the mood of reckoning with the death of children and of the poet herself. It is tempting to see the final lines of the sequence as a grace note: "this earth, this garden, this woman, / this one precious, perishable kingdom."

Yet Clifton kept writing; this is what true writers do. There are three other chief sources for this last set of poems that we have included, all in different stages of completion, but all also in clean condition—suggestive if not of being final, then of no longer being "in progress" to the extent that some other drafts are.

The first source of the last poems includes what I out of habit call "daybooks," but might more properly be called day planners, several of which are found among her papers at Emory. These eight-by-eleven inch, month-by-month calendars include her busy schedule of readings, and often serve as a kind of portable desk, with work memos, invitations to read, and travel itineraries tucked in; they also include drafts of poems in progress and what appear to be reading copies of new poems. Several poems in the "Last Poems & Drafts" section come from these daybooks, either in typed or occasionally handwritten form. The title "Book of Days" seems all the more fitting given this practice.

The poem "some points along some of the meridians" is a find from her 2007 daybook—it is immediately proceeded by a printed set of "point references" to what might be acupuncture or other localized medicines based on the body, the list a gift from a friend on her birthday. From this follows the "meridians" poem which at first seems merely a further list—but much like the poem that begins *The Book of Light*, consisting of merely the dictionary definition of light, there seems a purposeful ordering to the sections and even in the new title. All poems question the idea of what makes up a poem, or they should—and none more than the list poem—but here you can see her poet's sensibility, whether in the ordering of the body or her love of it, expressed through language. How poignant for someone at this time struggling with her health, and with an organ transplant, to call the kidney "deep valley" and "spirit storehouse" and "spirit burial ground." In this way, these last poems have not only survived, they are poems of a survivor.

The more immediately recognizable style of "6/27/06 seventy"—the date and age of her birthday—recasts a poem of a similar title that appears in *Voices*. The poem was written, we know, from early drafts in 2006 and appears completed in 2008. Like many of the last poems, Clifton started this on the computer: often not using her computer's word processing program, but e-mail, which appears to have provided less in the way of interfering "autocorrections"—capitalizing every "i" we can only imagine—with the directness of her old typewriter. Or even her Videowriter, a machine made only for word processing whose small screen may have impacted her line in ways we haven't quite fully understood—much as we haven't yet understood the ways the spirit writing impacted her work, with its different kind of daily log and practice, filled with connected, looping words from the pen never leaving the page. She often turned this page horizontally, like a landscape; the result is a quite different effect than those short, relineated "Ones" in *Mercy*.

While her computers are undergoing the kinds of forensics and archival investigations that may yet yield other poems—not to mention drafts of those poems we have here—processing this kind of "born digital" work is still underway. However, a number of poems here were clearly composed in e-mail then printed, including "6/27/06 seventy" and "after the children died."

Another set of her late work comes from Squaw Valley workshops in California. I taught at one session with her in 2005; as attendees to that conference know, all poets there, including workshop leaders, write a poem a day, handed out in the morning and workshopped that same day. Clifton, who attended the conference many times (and commented on the awkwardness of its place name), often used the daily practice to full advantage—indeed, a number of poems from *Voices* appear to have taken first form, or perhaps been polished further, at

Squaw Valley. The poems "haiku" and "An American Story" stem from files from that conference.

These poems may be the start of the project that Alexia Clifton remembers her mother mentioning toward what would be the end of her life: a book to be called *God Bless America*. While we have not yet encountered the full manuscript, the typescript three-line version of "God Bless America" we do have is far more than a fragment. Rather, like her "haiku," Clifton seems to be moving by suggestion. She was always one whose questions and love of paradox informed her best poems, like "why some people be mad at me sometimes":

> they ask me to remember
> but they want me to remember
> their memories
> and i keep on remembering
> mine.

The poem "God Bless America" was found among her last daybook, from 2010, where it was tucked in the short days of February, the month she would die in—fifty-one years to the day after her own mother. Right behind that poem is another poem, what appears to be the last poem Clifton wrote and the last poem in this book. There are two handwritten drafts to this poem that starts "In the middle of the Eye"; the second one, reprinted here as is, appears remarkably clean and direct. Prescient and powerful, the poem is both a testimony and an example of Clifton's strength to the end; she not only stands, but withstands, and stands up amidst "the fiery sight."

The last words in the 2010 daybook are the start to the acceptance speech Clifton began for the Frost Medal she was to be awarded by the Poetry Society of America in April of that year. While she did not live to give that speech, we still have her spoken, written, near sung voice in lines echoing her most reprinted poem: "I stand here before you having survived 3 bouts with cancer, a kidney transplant, the loss of my husband and two of my children and arthritis like you wouldn't believe. Indeed won't you celebrate with me?"

—Kevin Young

Lucille Clifton Bibliography

*Ordered chronologically, this bibliography accounts for first editions of all published books and limited editions by Lucille Clifton, including **poetry** (noted in bold), children's books, and memoir. All genres other than poetry are identified in parentheses, including a selection of broadsides. Thanks to Amy Hildreth Chen for her help with the bibliography.*

What Watches Me? A Writing and Drawing Book for You. (Children's Book) Washington, DC: US Dept. Health, Education & Welfare and the Central Atlantic Regional Educational Laboratory, c. 1968. This spiral-bound booklet of Clifton's rhyming set of riddles was written for schoolchildren who were meant to illustrate it. Apparently limited to 40 copies.

"Mae Baby." (Short Story) *Highlights for Children* (February 1969): 28-9. Clifton's first national magazine appearance.

Good Times. The Massachusetts Review Signature Series of Poets 4 (Winter 1969): 82-96. Separate offprint that includes sixteen poems from the forthcoming book Good Times.

Good Times. New York, NY: Random House, 1969. The book appeared in November.

The Black B C's. (Children's Book) New York, NY: E. P. Dutton & Co., 1970.

Some of the Days of Everett Anderson. (Children's Book) New York, NY: Holt, Rinehart, and Winston, 1970.

Good News About the Earth. New York, NY: Random House, 1972.

All Us Come Cross the Water. (Children's Book) New York, NY: Henry Holt & Co., 1973.

Don't You Remember? (Children's Book) New York, NY: E. P. Dutton & Co., 1973.

Good, Says Jerome. (Children's Book) New York, NY: E. P. Dutton & Co., 1973.

An Ordinary Woman. New York, NY: Random House, 1974.

"Three Wishes," *Free To Be…You and Me*, ed. Francine Klagsbrun. (New York: McGraw-Hill, 1974), 114. Clifton won an Emmy Award for the television broadcast of this popular program.

Everett Anderson's Year. (Children's Book) New York, NY: Holt, Rinehart and Winston, 1974.

The Times They Used to Be. (Children's Book) New York, NY: Holt, Rinehart, and Winston, 1974.

"All of Us Are All of Us." (Broadside) Detroit, MI: Broadside Press, March 1974. Broadside Series No. 81.

My brother fine with me. (Children's Book) New York, NY: Holt, Rinehart, and Winston, 1975.

Generations: A Memoir. New York, NY: Random House, 1976.

Five Magic Words. (Children's Book) Randallstown, MD: The Agnihotra Press, 1976. "Pictures by Sidney Clifton."

Everett Anderson's Friend. (Children's Book) New York, NY: Holt, Rinehart, and Winston, 1976.

Amifika. (Children's Book) New York, NY: E .P. Dutton, 1977.

The Boy Who Didn't Believe in Spring. (Children's Book) New York, NY: E. P. Dutton, 1978.

Everett Anderson's Nine Month Long. (Children's Book) New York, NY: Holt, Rinehart, and Winston, 1978.

Two-Headed Woman. Amherst, MA: University of Massachusetts Press, 1980.

My Friend Jacob. (Young Adult) New York, NY: Dutton Juvenile, 1980.

Sonora Beautiful. (Young Adult) New York, NY: Dutton Juvenile, 1981.

"Here is aanother bone to pick with you." (Broadside) Iowa City, IA: Toothpaste Press, 1981.

Everett Anderson's Goodbye. (Children's Book) New York, NY: Holt, Rinehart, and Winston, 1983.

The Lucky Stone. (Young Adult) New York, NY: Delacourt Press, 1986.

"Let There Be New Flowering." (Broadside) New York, NY: New York City Transit Authority, 1987.

Good Woman: Poems and a Memoir: 1969–1980. Brockport, NY: BOA Editions, Ltd. 1987.

Next: New Poems. **Brockport, NY: BOA Editions, 1987.**

Ten Oxherding Pictures. **(limited edition) Santa Cruz, CA: Moving Parts Press, 1988. Two hundred copies, thirty of which are numbered and signed.**

Quilting: 1987–1990. **Brockport, NY: BOA Editions, Ltd. 1991.**

Everett Anderson's Christmas Coming. (Children's Book) New York, NY: Henry Holt & Co., 1991.

Three Wishes. (Children's Book) New York, NY: Doubleday Book for Young Readers, 1992.

Everett Anderson's 1-2-3. (Children's Book) New York, NY: Henry Holt & Co., 1992.

The Book of Light. Port Townsend, WA: Copper Canyon Press, 1993.

The Terrible Stories. Brockport, NY: BOA Editions, Ltd., 1996.

Selected Poems. (Limited Edition) Minneapolis, MN: Tunheim Santrizos Company/Minnesota Center for the Arts, 1996. Print run of around 400 copies not for sale.

The Terrible Stories. London: Slow Dancer Publications, 1998. British edition.

"At the Cemetery, Walnut Grove Plantation, South Carolina, 1989." (Broadside). Wells College Press, 1998.

Blessing the Boats: New and Selected Poems. Rochester, NY: BOA Editions, Ltd., 2000. National Book Award winner.

One of the Problems of Everett Anderson. (Children's Book) New York, NY: Henry Holt & Co., 2001.

Mercy. 2004. Rochester, NY: BOA Editions, Ltd., 2004.

"Surely I Am Able to Write Poems." (Broadside) Kent, OH: Kent State University, 2004.

"Blood." (Broadside) Chicago, IL: Poetry Center of Chicago, 2004.

"Aunt Jemima." (Broadside) Atlanta, GA: Emory University, 2006. Printed letterpress by Littoral Press, Oakland, CA.

"Mulberry Fields." (Broadside) Chicago, IL: Poetry Foundation, 2007.

from the fenceless field. Rochester, NY: BOA Editions, Ltd., 2007. Promotional pamphlet including the poems "why some people be mad at my sometimes," "faith, "lu 1942," "in amira's room," "aunt jemima," "cream of wheat," "horse prayer," "raccoon prayer," "sorrows," and *"won't you celebrate with me."*

Voices. Rochester, NY: BOA Editions, Ltd., 2008.

"Study the Masters." (Broadside) New Haven, CT: Yale Collection of American Literature Reading Series, 2008.

Index of Poems

Titled poems are shown in roman. Untitled poems are indicated by their first line and appear in italics. First lines beginning with *a*, *an*, or *the* are alphabetized under *A* or *T.*

About the Co-Editors

Kevin Young is the author of seven books of poetry, including *Ardency: A Chronicle of the* Amistad *Rebels* (Knopf, 2011) and *Jelly Roll* (Knopf, 2003), which was a finalist for the National Book Award and won the Paterson Poetry Prize. His first book, *Most Way Home* (William Morrow, 1995), was selected by Lucille Clifton for the National Poetry Series and went on to win the Zacharis First Book Award from *Ploughshares*.

He is the editor of seven other collections, including *The Art of Losing: Poems of Grief & Healing*, *Best American Poetry 2011*, *The Hungry Ear: Poems of Food & Drink*, and *Selected Poems: John Berryman* for the Library of America. Young's book *The Grey Album: On the Blackness of Blackness* won the Graywolf Press Nonfiction Prize and appeared March 2012.

Young is the Atticus Haygood Professor of Creative Writing and English and Curator of Literary Collections and the Raymond Danowski Poetry Library at Emory University in Atlanta, where Clifton's papers are housed.

Michael S. Glaser is a Professor Emeritus at St. Mary's College of Maryland where he served as both a professor and an administrator for nearly forty years. He is a recipient of the Homer Dodge Endowed Award for Excellence in Teaching; the Columbia Merit Award from the Poetry Committee of the Greater Washington, D.C. area for his service to poetry; and the Andrew White Medal for his dedication to the intellectual and scholarly life, and for his commitment to sustaining the poetic tradition in the State of Maryland. Glaser served as a Maryland State Arts Council poet-in-the-schools for over twenty years and is a member of the Board of Directors of the Maryland Humanities Council. He served as Poet Laureate of Maryland from 2004 through 2009.

His early works include *A Lover's Eye* (The Bunny & Crocodile Press, 1989), and *In the Men's Room and Other Poems*, which was the winner of the 1996 Painted Bride Quarterly chapbook competition. His most recent collections of poems include *Being a Father*, which was published in July 2004; the chapbook *Fire Before the Hands*, which won the Anabiosis Press, 2007 chapbook prize; and *Disrupting Consensus*, which won the Teacher's Voice chapbook competition and was published in December 2009. Glaser has also edited three anthologies: *The Cooke Book* (1989), *Weavings 2000: The Maryland Millennial Anthology*, and a memorial tribute to Lucille Clifton, *Come Celebrate with Me* (2011).

Born in Chicago, Illinois, Glaser received his B.A. from Denison University and his M.A. and Ph.D. from Kent State University. He lives in St. Mary's City with his wife, the educator Kathleen W. Glaser, who works with the Center for Courage and Renewal. He is the proud father of five grown children, Brian, Joshua, Daniel, Amira, and Eva, and nine grandchildren.

About Lucille Clifton

> oh children
> think about the good times
> —*Good Times*, 1969

Lucille Clifton was one of the most distinguished, decorated, and beloved poets of her time. She won the National Book Award for Poetry, and was the first Black female recipient of the Ruth Lilly Poetry Prize for lifetime achievement. Ms. Clifton received many additional honors throughout her career, beginning with the Discovery Award from the New York YW/YMHA Poetry Center in 1969 for her first volume *Good Times*, and including a 1976 Emmy Award for Outstanding Writing for the television special "Free to Be You and Me," a Lannan Literary Award in 1994, and the Robert Frost Medal in 2010. Her honors and awards give testament to the universality of her unique and resonant voice. She was named a Literary Lion by the New York Public Library in 1996, served as a Chancellor of the Academy of American Poets from 1999 to 2005, and was elected a fellow in Literature of the American Academy of Arts and Sciences. In 1987, she became the first author to have two books of poetry—*Good Woman* and *Next*—chosen as finalists for the Pulitzer Prize in the same year. She was also the author of eighteen children's books, and in 1984 received the Coretta Scott King Award from the American Library Association for her book *Everett Anderson's Good-bye*.

Born June 27, 1936, in Depew, New York, Lucille Clifton lived in Buffalo, New York, from her early childhood until 1967 when she moved to Baltimore with her husband Fred and their six children: Sidney, Fredrica, Channing, Gillian, Graham, and Alexia. Her first book of poetry, *Good Times*, was published in 1969, shortly after her work had been introduced to Langston Hughes by her close friend Ishmael Reed. From 1969 to 1974 her poems and essays appeared in popular publications of the time, including *The Negro Digest* and *Ms.* magazine. She was appointed Maryland's Poet Laureate in 1974 and remained in that post for eleven years. After her husband's death in 1984, she moved to Santa Cruz, California, having been offered a professorship at University of California at Santa Cruz. Ms. Clifton taught at numerous colleges and universities, beginning at Coppin State College in Baltimore (1974–77) and including the University of California at Santa Cruz (1984–89), Memphis State University (1994–1995), Duke University, where she served for several terms as the William Blackburn Distinguished Visiting Professor (1998–99), and Dartmouth College (2007). Beginning in 1989, Ms. Clifton taught at St. Mary's College of Maryland, where she served as Distinguished Professor of Humanities until her retirement in 2006. She was inducted into Phi Beta Kappa and received seven honorary doctorate degrees.

Lucille Clifton's integrity and moral voice about matters in our individual and communal lives served many as a beacon of courage and compassion. Her poems, forged from experience, emotion, and a fierce, truth-telling intellect, focus on the human struggle for dignity, justice, and freedom. As the citation from the National Book Awards so accurately asserts, her poems, "fueled by emotional necessity . . . [achieve] such clarity and power that her vision becomes representative, communal, and unforgettable." Lucille, in her life and in her poetry, dwelt in the possibilities that truth redeems, that always there is hope. Her poetry engages its reader with the deeper and more complex truths of our lives, and it does so with such clarity that even the radical ambiguity within which we live seems filled with light.

Lucille's great courage and strength shine through her poems. Even when she wrote about personally difficult subject matter, she approached the world with infinite interest and tenderness toward the mystery of all that lives. Having survived sexual molestation, the loss of her home, and the deaths of her mother, husband, and two children, she forged a poetry that served as solace, explanation, redemption, and prayer for both herself and her audience. Ms. Clifton died on February 13, 2010, on the fifty-first anniversary of her mother's death.

> And I could tell you about things we been through, some awful ones, some wonderful, but I know that the things that make us are more than that, our lives are more than the days in them, our lives are our line and we go on. . . .
>
> —*Generations*, 1976

BOA Editions, Ltd. American Poets Continuum Series

Colophon

The publication of this book was made possible by the generous support of the
Lannan Foundation

as well as contributions by the following major donors
Joseph Belluck
Gwen & Gary Conners
the Gouvernet Arts Fund
Robert & Willy Hursh
Ellen Conroy Kennedy
Wendy & James Mnookin
the Mary. S. Mulligan Charitable Trust
Rochester Institute of Technology
St. Mary's College of Maryland
the BOA Editions, Ltd. Board of Directors

additional support from the following patrons
the Ames-Amzalak Memorial Trust
Liz Axelrod
Michael Hall
Dorianne Laux & Joseph Millar
Deborah Ronnen & Sherman Levey
Richard & Vicki Schwartz
Patricia & Michael Wilder
Bruce Willard
Dr. Ian Wilson

and the kind sponsorship of the following individuals

Anonymous	Jack & Gail Langerak
Anonymous, *in memory of Greg Lippard*	Katherine Lederer
Kazim Ali & Marco Wilkinson	John & Barbara Lovenheim
Nathalie Andrews	Robert & Francie Marx
Jeanne Marie Beaumont	Edith Matthai, *in memory of Peter Hursh*
Deborah Brown	Michael McDonough
Bernadette Catalana	Carol McKenna & Matt Belanger
Mark & Karen Conners	Werner K. & Charles G. Postler
Peter & Karen Conners	Boo Poulin,
Anne Coon & Craig Zicari	*in honor of Sandi Henchel*
Jim Daniels	*in honor of Susan Burke & Bill Leonardi*
Susan DeWitt Davie	John Roche
Peter & Suzanne Durant	Cindy Rogers
Jonathan Everitt	Steven O. Russell & Phyllis Rifkin-Russell
Suressa & Richard Forbes	David W. Ryon
Anne Germanacos	Jane Schuster,
Jacquie & Andy Germanow	*in memory of Anthony Piccione*
Aracelis Girmay	Rob Tortorella
Robert L. Giron	Justin L. Vigdor
Howard Haims & Carole Cooper-Haims	David & Ellen Wallack
William B. Hauser	Michael Waters & Mihaela Moscaliuc
Peg Heminway	Nan & Dan Westervelt,
Robin, Hollon & Casey Hursh	*in honor of Pat Braus & Ed Lopez*
X. J. & Dorothy M. Kennedy	Glenn & Helen William
Laurie Kutchins